DEFEATING THOSE DRAGONS

DEFEATING THOSE DRAGONS

8 sessions on overcoming hindrances to our spiritual growth

by David P. Seemuth

VICTOR BOOKS®

A DIVISION OF SCRIPTURE PRESS PUBLICATIONS INC.
USA CANADA ENGLAND

Scripture quotations are taken from the *Holy Bible, New International Version,* © 1973, 1978, 1984, International Bible Society. Used by permission of Zondervan Bible Publishers.

Recommended Dewey Decimal Classification: 301.402
Suggested Subject Heading: SMALL GROUPS

Library of Congress Catalog Card Number: 91-65455
ISBN: 0-89693-924-3

 2   3   4   5   6   7   8   9   10 Printing / Year   95   94   93   92

VICTOR BOOKS
A division of SP Publications, Inc.
        Wheaton, Illinois 60187

CONTENTS

PURPOSE: To gain the insight, support, and experience needed to overcome hindrances to our spiritual lives.

INTRODUCTION

Defeating Those Dragons is for people who want to examine some of the hindrances in their lives which prevent them from attaining spiritual growth and maturity. An in-depth Leader's Guide is included at the back of the book with suggested time guidelines to help you structure your emphases. Each of the 8 sessions contains the following elements:

❑ **GroupSpeak**—quotes from group members that capsulize what the session is about.

❑ **Getting Acquainted**—activities or selected readings to help you begin thinking and sharing from your life and experiences about the subject of the session. Use only those options that seem appropriate for your group.

❑ **Gaining Insight**—questions and in-depth Bible study help you gain principles from Scripture for life-related application.

❑ **Growing By Doing**—an opportunity to practice the Truth learned in the Gaining Insight section.

❑ **Going The Second Mile**—a personal enrichment section for you to do on your own.

❑ **Growing As A Leader**—an additional section in the Leader's Guide for the development and assessment of leadership skills.

❑ **Pocket Principles**—brief guidelines inserted in the Leader's Guide to help the Group Leader learn small group leadership skills as needed.

❑ **Session Objectives**—goals listed in the Leader's Guide that describe what should happen in the group by the end of session.

IS THIS YOUR FIRST SMALL GROUP?

'smol grüp: A limited number of individuals assembled together having some unifying relationship.

Kris'chən   4–12 persons who meet together on a regular ba-
'smol grüp: sis,
over a determined period of time, for the shared purpose of pursuing biblical truth. They seek to mature in Christ and become equipped to serve as His ministers in the world.

Picture Your First Small Group.

List some words that describe what you want your small group to look like.

What Kind Of Small Group Do You Have?

People form all kinds of groups based on gender, age, marital status, and so forth. There are advantages and disadvantages to each. Here are just a few:

❑ **Same Age Groups** will probably share similar needs and interests.

❑ **Intergenerational Groups** bring together people with different perspectives and life experiences.

❑ **Men's or Women's Groups** usually allow greater freedom in sharing and deal with more focused topics.

❑ **Singles or Married Groups** determine their relationship emphases based on the needs of a particular marital status.

❑ **Mixed Gender Groups** (**singles and/or couples**) stimulate interaction and broaden viewpoints while reflecting varied lifestyles.

However, the most important area of "alikeness" to consider when forming a group is an **agreed-on purpose**. Differences in purpose will sabotage your group and keep its members from bonding. If, for example, Mark wants to pray but not play while Jan's goal is to learn through playing, then Mark and Jan's group will probably not go anywhere. People need different groups at different times in their lives. Some groups will focus on sharing and accountability, some on work projects or service, and others on worship. *Your small group must be made up of persons who have similar goals.*

How Big Should Your Small Group Be?
The **fewest** people to include would be **4**. Accountability will be high, but absenteeism may become a problem.

The **most** to include would be **12**. But you will need to subdivide regularly into groups of 3 or 4 if you want people to feel cared for and to have time for sharing.

How Long Should You Meet?
8 Weeks gives you a start toward becoming a close community, but doesn't overburden busy schedules. Count on needing three or four weeks to develop a significant trust level. The smaller the group, the more quickly trust develops.

Weekly Meetings will establish bonding at a good pace and allow for accountability. The least you can meet and still be an effective group is once a month. If you choose the latter, work at individual contact among group members between meetings.

You will need **75 minutes** to accomplish a quality meeting. The larger the size, the more time it takes to become a healthy group. Serving refreshments will add 20–30 minutes, and singing and/or prayer time, another 20–30 minutes. Your time duration may be determined by the time of day you meet and by the amount of energy members bring to the group. Better to start small and ask for more time when it is needed because of growth.

What Will Your Group Do?

To be effective, each small group meeting should include:

1. **Sharing** — You need to share who you are and what is happening in your life. This serves as a basis for relationship building and becomes a springboard for searching out scriptural truth.

2. **Scripture** — There must always be biblical input from the Lord to teach, rebuke, correct, and train in right living. Such material serves to move your group in the direction of maturity in Christ and protects from pooled ignorance and distorted introspection.

3. **Truth in practice** — It is vital to provide opportunities for *doing* the Word of God. Experiencing this within the group insures greater likelihood that insights gained will be utilized in everyday living.

Other elements your group may wish to add to these three are: a time of **worship, specific prayer** for group members, **shared projects**, a time to **socialize** and enjoy **refreshments**, and **recreation.**

ONE

Winning Over Worry

GroupSpeak: *"It seems I can't get away from these nagging thoughts. So often I am convinced that something has gone wrong or something terrible has happened. But seldom am I right."*

The Dragon of Worry

Most of us can attest to having occasional thoughts of worry and concern. If a beloved family member doesn't arrive at a designated hour we grow concerned. And such concern is reasonable—unless it is carried to the extreme. It would be wrong to phone the Highway Patrol if a person is a few minutes late. Sometimes, though, we are plagued with excessive worry. Such worry we know goes far beyond the realm of the reasonable. In this session, we will attack the dragon of worry since it saps the strength from us and clouds reason.

 GETTING ACQUAINTED

A Snapshot of Your Day

If a television video crew followed you around yesterday and captured your life on camera, what are the kinds of events the public would see?

Was there anything unusual about your routine before you began your tasks for the day?

What was the most important event of the day?

Did anything frustrate you?

What did you do in the evening?

There was probably some occasion during your day when things did not go 100 percent according to your perceived plan. Did anything happen that caused you to be concerned?

How do you know when concerns progress to anxiety or worry?

What are the reasons for your worry and anxiety today?

If you could produce a worry list, or an anxiety list, what would be on it? What kinds of things do you worry about?

Worry List

How does the world around us add to our discontent?

What items on your list are made worse because of the pressures of society?

GAINING INSIGHT

Scripture Study
Read Philippians 4:4-14.

⁴Rejoice in the Lord always. I will say it again: Rejoice! ⁵Let your gentleness be evident to all. The Lord is near. ⁶Do not be anxious about anything, but in everything, by prayer and petition, with thanksgiving, present your requests to God. ⁷And the peace of God, which transcends all understanding, will guard your hearts and your minds in Christ Jesus.

⁸Finally, brothers, whatever is true, whatever is noble, whatever is right, whatever is pure, whatever is lovely, whatever is admirable—if anything is excellent or praiseworthy—think about such things. ⁹Whatever you have learned or received or heard from me, or seen in me—put it into practice. And the God of peace will be with you.

¹⁰I rejoice greatly in the Lord that at last you have renewed your concern for me. Indeed, you have been concerned, but you had no opportunity to show it. ¹¹I am not saying this because I am in need, for I have learned to be content whatever the circumstances. ¹²I know what it is to be in need, and I know what it is to have plenty. I have learned the secret of being content in any and every situation, whether well fed or hungry, whether living in plenty

or in want. ¹³I can do everything through Him who gives me strength.

¹⁴Yet it was good of you to share in my troubles.

Philippians 4:4-14

The Apostle Paul was imprisoned when he wrote the Epistle to the Philippian believers. He knew that he might be executed during his stay. On the surface he had every reason to be anxious, even despairing. Yet joy is one of the characteristics of this little letter. Contentment characterized his demeanor. He had many reasons to complain, but he didn't. We can certainly learn from Paul's experience how to find contentment when things aren't going well or even when things seem to be going just fine.

One of the commands Paul gave in this section is *rejoice.* We don't use this word much in modern speech. What terms are used today for the word *rejoice?*

In what ways does rejoicing diminish anxiety?

How do we actually go about rejoicing?

Since Paul repeated his command to rejoice in verse 4, he must have had a good reason for writing this to the Philippian believers. This is not merely positive thinking, but it includes thinking positively about how God has worked in our lives.

According to verses 6-7, what is another antidote to anxiety?

Why are verses 6-7 so difficult to practice?

We must not forget that Paul promised that we might have the peace of God in the midst of such difficulties. Paul himself knew this kind of experience as he dealt with the problem of his thorn in the flesh in 2 Corinthians 12:1-10. But God gave him the ability to live through such a difficult experience.

Notice Paul's attitude in verses 11-12. Summarize it in your own words.

Notice that Paul urged the Philippian believers to follow through on their concern for him. It would have been easy for Paul to ask them to send the money immediately. However, he used the situation as a time for teaching.

There is a secret to this attitude. Paul reveals this mystery in verse 13. How does verse 13 provide us with the ultimate answer to our anxieties?

Can you see how God can sustain you through the most difficult of times when worry seems to be the only option? Recognizing God's ultimate control, power, and love is the path to contentment.

GROWING BY DOING

Attacking The Dragon
Review your Worry List of anxiety producers. How can you diminish the anxiety over these issues using the principles Paul presented to the Philippian believers?

What can you be rejoicing in as a way of diminishing anxiety?

How can we encourage each other to maintain this sense of joy in the midst of our concerns?

Levels of Contentment
Rate your level of contentment in each of the following areas:

Your "job" right now?

poor 1 2 3 4 5 6 7 8 9 great

Your finances?

poor 1 2 3 4 5 6 7 8 9 great

Your family situation?

poor 1 2 3 4 5 6 7 8 9 great

Other areas of life _____?

poor 1 2 3 4 5 6 7 8 9 great

Which one of these could you share with the group for support and prayer?

GOING THE SECOND MILE

Thinking About Your Group
Did someone share a particular concern which struck you as needing immediate prayer? Who was that person?

How can you pray for him or her?

Thinking About Yourself
Is there an area of your life that you must learn to be content with?

How can you combat discontentedness and anxiety with Paul's philosophy of life?

Thinking About Your World
With whom can you share what you learned about anxiety?

Is there someone you know who is particularly affected by anxiety and worry?

How can you share Paul's principles with that person?

TWO

Freedom from Fear

GroupSpeak: *"The doctor said it was something that can be corrected very easily with surgery. When it comes down to it, I guess I am afraid of what may happen."*

The Dragon of Fear

Children often feel free to communicate their feelings. It is not unusual for little Jenny to want her mom or dad to hold her when she sees a scary television show or hears a suspicious noise. It is refreshing to see such innocence and openness in children.

Adults don't often share that same openness. Rather than facing fear, we often suppress it. Rather than asking for comfort, we ignore it. Instead of looking closely at unnerving events or situations, we prefer to turn our attention elsewhere. If we were to examine the events of our day, what would we say could inspire a sense of fear?

Have you ever waited for the results of a lab test? It can be very disconcerting. Every phone call brings expectations. Thoughts of mortal illnesses flood the mind. When the phone rings, we anticipate receiving either bad news or good news. When it is only Aunt Millie calling to chat, we are frustrated because she is tying up the line.

21

Uncertainty is just one of the causes for fear in our lives. There are many other catalysts for fear. Yet God would have us lead lives that are characterized by freedom from debilitating fear.

In this session, we will look at some antidotes for fear. We will examine Joshua's experience as he began his career as the head of Israel. In a situation that could have led to tremendous fear, God provided enough for Joshua to alleviate the fears that were faced by the Israelites.

 ## GETTING ACQUAINTED

Fears And Phobias
Do you identify with any of the following phobias, whether mildly or greatly? Are there items you would add to this list?

- ❏ Fear of heights
- ❏ Fear of dogs
- ❏ Fear of being alone
- ❏ Fear of flying
- ❏ Fear of crowds
- ❏ Fear of failure
- ❏ Fear of doctors and dentists

Which of these could you share with the group to give them a brief look of one thing that might cause a certain amount of fear within you?

What significant events from your past have caused you to be fearful?

Why do you think we prefer not to look at these events squarely in the eye?

22

In what ways does our society deal with such fear?

We usually feel fearful when we are threatened. Make a list of those things that threaten you and cause fear.

 ## GAINING INSIGHT

Scripture Study
Read Joshua 1:1-18.

¹**After the death of Moses the servant of the LORD, the LORD said to Joshua son of Nun, Moses' aide: ²"Moses my servant is dead. Now then, you and all these people, get ready to cross the Jordan River into the land I am about to give to them—to the Israelites. ³I will give you every place where you set your foot, as I promised Moses. ⁴Your territory will extend from the desert to Lebanon, and from the great river, the Euphrates—all the Hittite country—to the Great Sea on the west. ⁵No one will be able to stand up against you all the days of your life. As I was with Moses, so I will be with you; I will never leave you nor forsake you.**

⁶**"Be strong and courageous, because you will lead these people to inherit the land I swore to their forefathers to give them. ⁷Be strong and very courageous. Be careful to obey all the law My servant Moses gave you; do not turn from it to the right or to the left, that you may be successful wherever you go. ⁸Do not let this Book of the Law depart from your mouth; meditate on it day and night, so that you may be careful to do everything written in it. Then you will be prosperous and successful. ⁹Have I not commanded you? Be strong and courageous. Do not be terrified; do not be discouraged, for the LORD your God will be with you wherever you go."**

¹⁰"So Joshua ordered the officers of the people: ¹¹"Go through the camp and tell the people, 'Get your supplies ready. Three days from now you will cross the Jordan here to go in and take possession of the land the LORD your God is giving you for your own.' "

¹²But to the Reubenites, the Gadites and the half-tribe of Manasseh, Joshua said, ¹³"Remember the command that Moses the servant of the LORD gave you: 'The LORD your God is giving you rest and has granted you this land.' ¹⁴Your wives, your children and your livestock may stay in the land that Moses gave you east of the Jordan, but all your fighting men, fully armed, must cross over ahead of your brothers. You are to help your brothers ¹⁵until the LORD gives them rest, as He has done for you, and until they too have taken possession of the land that the LORD your God is giving them. After that, you may go back and occupy your own land, which Moses the servant of the LORD gave you east of the Jordan toward the sunrise."

¹⁶Then they answered Joshua, "Whatever you have commanded us we will do, and wherever you send us we will go. ¹⁷Just as we fully obeyed Moses, so we will obey you. Only may the LORD your God be with you as He was with Moses. ¹⁸Whoever rebels against your word and does not obey your words, whatever you may command them, will be put to death. Only be strong and courageous!"

Joshua 1:1-18

If Israel had an organizational chart, we would see that Joshua was in an enviable position in Israelite society. Moses, Israel's designated leader during the time of the Exodus, chose Joshua as his right-hand man to assist him in ushering the stubborn Israelites through the wilderness to the Promised Land. Years earlier, Joshua had spied out the new land and brought back a report saying: "The land we passed through and explored is exceedingly good. If the LORD is pleased with us, He will lead us into that land, a land flowing with milk and honey, and will give it to us" (Numbers 14:7-8).

Joshua was the perfect candidate for the second-in-command role, but as often happens, those who are second-in-command are thrust into the chief executive position through events beyond their control. Joshua was promoted as a result of Moses' death. Imagine the feelings of fear and anxiety that Joshua must have experienced stepping into Moses' sandals. As we look at Joshua 1, we will see how God dealt with Joshua's fear and timidity, and how He can deal with us in the midst of fearful times.

List several of the commands that God gave Joshua.

Why do you think God had to remind Joshua to be strong and courageous? Was there anything that Joshua had to fear? What were the tasks that had to be done? What lay ahead of Joshua and his countrymen?

Now that we have identified the commands that God had given Moses, let's identify the many promises that God gave him.

First of all, what did God promise about His presence?

Second, what did God promise to do for Joshua in verses 3-6?

Third, what did God give Joshua to help him in his new role as chief of the Israelite army?

What does this Book of the Law in verse 8 represent for the believer? How can God alleviate some of our fears through the use of this resource?

There is another aspect that we often forget as we confront situations that make us fearful—God is in control. If God is the author of history and He controls human events, how should we view scary situations?

 GROWING BY DOING

Attacking The Dragon
What are those things in your life right now that could cause you a sense of fear? Inadequacy as a parent or spouse? Insecurity? Your job performance? List several situations right now that might cause you to be afraid.

How can you appropriate the gifts God has given you as described in Joshua 1?

Which gift do you need most?

❏ God's presence?
❏ God's promises?
❏ God's providence?

26

Which of these is most meaningful to you right now? Why?

Which of these will you need to ponder more fully in the coming week?

How can knowing God's presence help us as we go through fearful events?

Why would knowing God's promises also help us navigate through difficult situations?

Notice that God gave Joshua a sense of partnership with the rest of God's people. The Israelites encouraged Joshua by saying, "Whatever you have commanded us we will do, and wherever you send us we will go. Just as we fully obeyed Moses, so we will obey you. Only may the LORD your God be with you as He was with Moses" (Joshua 1:16-17). The people of God can stand with us in our fears whatever they may be. Spend some time right now praying for one another, for the particular fears group members may be going through.

GOING THE SECOND MILE

Thinking About Your Group
Is there someone in the group who is going through a crisis which could lead to a great deal of fear? Who?

Which of God's gifts, as we have outlined them, would be most appropriate to remind that person about?

How can you encourage that person? With a letter? A phone call? A visit?

Thinking About Yourself
Identify your #1 fear.

How can you attack this dragon, now that you know about God's empowering and gifting?

Thinking about your world, what are those situations that you see taking place in your world today that create a sense of fear? How can you pray for those people who are living with those fears? Write a prayer right now for those suffering from intense fears.

Dear God,

THREE

Overcoming Temptation

GroupSpeak: *"Sometimes I feel like I just can't get away from the desire to do wrong. It's like I'm assaulted with thoughts I know are not pleasing to God."*

The Dragon of Temptation

Many years ago on a television show called "Laugh In," comedian Flip Wilson explained his questionable behavior with the excuse, "The devil made me do it!" Times have changed but, if we consulted with various psychologists and therapists, we would find blame for problems and failures being placed on the individual's environment, parents, and/or socioeconomic background.

Without discounting legitimate uses of psychology and therapy, we shouldn't be too quick to place the responsibility for common weaknesses and failures exclusively at Satan's feet or on the shoulders of our parents. As human beings we inevitably encounter temptations. Our backgrounds often dictate how we react to those temptations, but it is our responsibility to act appropriately.

In John 8:34-36, Jesus told the Pharisees, "I tell you the truth, everyone who sins is a slave to sin. Now a slave has no permanent place in the family, but a son belongs to it forever.

31

So if the Son sets you free, you will be free indeed." It is the right of the believer to be free from the bondage of sin. Indeed, Jesus promises that we will be free if we dedicate ourselves to Him. Too many of us fall short of experiencing freedom from sin, because we have not come to grips with how to handle temptation. In this session, we will look at the way Jesus handled temptations from Satan and through His model we will find a strategy to defeat this dragon.

GETTING ACQUAINTED

Excuses, Excuses, Excuses
In our culture, we rarely see either a national political figure or a very prominent business executive admit mistakes or even illegalities. It seems far easier to cover up those mistakes or simply ignore their existence.

We need to recognize that we live in a world where there are ample opportunities for succumbing to temptations and failing to live up to what we ought to be. Still, we feel pressured to put the blame elsewhere.

Why do we have difficulties with temptations?

What is a temptation?

What sorts of temptations do you think the following people face?

❑ a politician in a campaign year
❑ an auto mechanic
❑ a checker at a supermarket
❑ a counselor
❑ a student
❑ a pastor

Identify one of your roles in life. What temptations might you face as you function in that role?

GAINING INSIGHT

Recognizing Temptation

In Galatians 5:19-21, we find a list of different works of the flesh or different sins that people may commit. While this list is not intended to be exhaustive, certainly it covers a breadth of sins that people commit. Read the following Scriptures.

> **¹⁹The acts of the sinful nature are obvious: sexual immorality, impurity and debauchery; ²⁰idolatry and witchcraft; hatred, discord, jealousy, fits of rage, selfish ambition, dissensions, factions ²¹and envy; drunkenness, orgies, and the like. I warn you, as I did before, that those who live like this will not inherit the kingdom of God.**
>
> **Galatians 5:19-21**

> **⁵For of this you can be sure: No immoral, impure or greedy person—such a man is an idolater—has any inheritance in the kingdom of Christ and of God.**
>
> **Ephesians 5:5**

How would you classify the areas of sin in the Galatians passage? See if you can classify them into four categories.

What other category might you add from Ephesians 5:5?

Is there a particular item in these passages that is unknown to you or not defined well in your mind? If so, write it down and look it up in a dictionary.

In what way is each of these sins a perversion of something that is good?

Read Matthew 4:1-11 and answer the following questions.

¹Then Jesus was led by the Spirit into the desert to be tempted by the devil. ²After fasting forty days and forty nights, He was hungry. ³The tempter came to Him and said, "If You are the Son of God, tell these stones to become bread."

⁴Jesus answered, "It is written: 'Man does not live on bread alone, but on every word that comes from the mouth of God.' "

⁵Then the devil took Him to the holy city and had Him stand on the highest point of the temple. ⁶"If you are the Son of God," he said, "throw yourself down. For it is written:

" 'He will command His angels concerning you, and they will lift you up in their hands, so that you will not strike your foot against a stone.' "

⁷Jesus answered him, "It is also written: 'Do not put the Lord your God to the test.' "

⁸Again, the devil took Him to a very high mountain and showed Him all the kingdoms of the world and their splendor. ⁹"All this I will give You," he said, "if You will bow down and worship me."

Jesus said to him, "Away from Me, Satan! For it is written: 'Worship the Lord your God, and serve Him only.' "

¹¹Then the devil left Him, and angels came and attended Him.

Matthew 4:1-11

The temptation of Jesus can be divided into three basic parts, but let us first examine why and how Jesus was tempted.

What is the setting for this temptation?

Many have pointed out that the temptation of Christ is in direct contrast with the temptation of Adam and Eve. In what way is the setting here in contrast with the setting of Adam and Eve?

What motivated Jesus to be in the wilderness at this point in His life?

In the first temptation Satan urged Jesus to change the stones to be bread. Why would this be a temptation for Jesus at this time?

What does Jesus' response tell you about the way Jesus used His power for His own needs?

In the second temptation, the devil challenged Jesus to use His power to draw a large following. How did Jesus respond to this temptation?

In what way did Jesus show that He would trust in God's plan and that He didn't need to test God's word?

In the third temptation, Jesus was urged to gain access to ruling the kingdom by worshiping Satan. How did Jesus respond to this aspect of temptation, and what was the root of the issue?

Read the following verses, looking for ways to deal with temptation.

¹³No temptation has seized you except what is common to man. And God is faithful; He will not let you be tempted beyond what you can bear. But when you are tempted, He will also provide a way out so that you can stand up under it.

1 Corinthians 10:13

⁵Put to death, therefore, whatever belongs to your earthly nature: sexual immorality, impurity, lust, evil desires and greed, which is idolatry.

Colossians 3:5

GROWING BY DOING

Attacking The Dragon

The categories that were identified earlier list what might be called our tendency areas of sin. Which of those tendencies would you say you have the most difficulty with? Is there a particular sin that seems to tempt you more than others?

How can you react properly to these areas of temptation?

In what way have you sensed God's strengthening in facing temptation?

Part of Satan's strategy is to convince us to rebel against God's grace, God's Word, or God's authority. In which of these areas do you most easily succumb to temptation?

How can your Christian brothers and sisters help you in your struggle against the various temptations in your life?

How can you be held accountable for resistance against sin?

In what way can you share your concern or your own weaknesses with other group members?

GOING THE SECOND MILE

Thinking About Your Group
Did anyone in our group seem touched very deeply by this session?

In what ways might you be able to be used by God to strengthen that group member? By helping him or her be accountable for making good decisions? By talking to the person?

Thinking About Yourself
Only you know the deepest areas of your life. You know where you've experienced a sense of victory or a sense of failure over temptations.

37

In what ways will you be tempted in the coming days, and how specifically will you prepare in advance to resist such temptation? What safeguards will you build into the next few days?

Thinking About Your World
Think of a political figure or other well-known celebrity who seems particularly vulnerable to different forms of temptation.

How can you pray for this person in the coming week?

FOUR

Defeating Discouragement

GroupSpeak: *"I feel so tired sometimes having to deal with the same pressures day in and day out. It almost seems pointless. I don't seem to be making any progress."*

The Dragon of Discouragement

People define *discouragement* in many different ways. For some, it's looking at their checkbook. For others, it's looking at their limited physical energy in the midst of disease. Still others would define *discouragement* as an exceedingly difficult relationship.

There is no question that we live in a world that is plagued by discouragement and despair. At times, life seems to present us with such great problems that we wonder how we will carry on. In the Scriptures, God speaks about encouragement and our responsibility to encourage one another.

In this session we will look at discouragement and identify principles to avoid it. We must not kid each other into thinking that discouragement can be totally avoided, but we can limit the onslaught of this particular dragon.

GETTING ACQUAINTED

Defining Discouragement

If you were to write a personal definition of the word *discouragement,* what might it include?

What are those ingredients that tend to bring discouragement into your life?

Are you particularly prone to discouragement? Or are you a person who tends to lead a fairly discourage-free life?

On a scale of 1–10 (1 meaning you aren't discouraged very often and 10 meaning you are discouraged quite a bit of the time), where would you rate yourself and why?

Seldom a   1 2 3 4 5 6 7 8 9 10   Often a
Discouraging   Discouraging
Word   Word

What do you do when you get discouraged? Call a friend? Sleep a lot? Go on a chocolate binge?

GAINING INSIGHT

Scripture Study

Elijah knew what it was like to be discouraged. Yet, if we were to review the story of Elijah, we would find that he had been used mightily by God on Mount Carmel.

Elijah went face-to-face with the prophets of Baal, the god of the Canaanites. Some of the Israelites had forsaken the true God and began worshiping Baal. So Elijah confronted the people.

²¹"How long will you waver between two opinions. If the LORD is God, follow Him. But if Baal is God, follow him."

But the people said nothing.

1 Kings 18:21

The people were stuck on the fence, so Elijah placed a clear choice before them. He suggested that the prophets of Baal call on their god to burn up the sacrifice they had prepared for him. But their shouting and violent self-abuse availed nothing. As the story continues, we find that Elijah mocked the prophets of Baal.

²⁷"Shout louder!" he said. "Surely he is a god! Perhaps he is deep in thought, or busy, or traveling. Maybe he is sleeping and must be awakened."

1 Kings 18:27

The turning point in this encounter came when God showed Himself to be the true God by consuming Elijah's sacrifice with fire. It was a dramatic showing of the power of God, and Elijah was viewed as the prophet extraordinaire of the Lord.

There is no question that Elijah must have felt encouraged by God's demonstration to the people. Acting on the authority of the Lord, he carried out the sentence for false prophets by killing over 400 prophets of Baal.

But only a short time later, we find that Elijah became greatly discouraged.

43

¹Now Ahab told Jezebel everything Elijah had done and how he had killed all the prophets with the sword. ²So Jezebel sent a messenger to Elijah to say, "May the gods deal with me, be it ever so severely, if by this time tomorrow I do not make your life like that of one of them."

Elijah was afraid and ran for his life. When he came to Beersheba in Judah, he left his servant there, ⁴while he himself went a day's journey into the desert. He came to a broom tree, sat down under it and prayed that he might die. "I have had enough, LORD," he said. "Take my life; I am no better than my ancestors." ⁵Then he lay down under the tree and fell asleep.

All at once an angel touched him and said, "Get up and eat." ⁶He looked around, and there by his head was a cake of bread baked over hot coals, and a jar of water. He ate and drank and then lay down again.

⁷The angel of the LORD came back a second time and touched him and said, "Get up and eat, for the journey is too much for you." ⁸So he got up and ate and drank. Strengthened by that food, he traveled forty days and forty nights until he reached Horeb, the mountain of God. ⁹There he went into a cave and spent the night.

And the word of the LORD came to him: "What are you doing here, Elijah?"

¹⁰He replied, "I have been very zealous for the LORD God Almighty. The Israelites have rejected Your covenant, broken down Your altars, and put Your prophets to death with the sword. I am the only one left, and now they are trying to kill me too."

¹¹The LORD said, "Go out and stand on the mountain in the presence of the LORD, for the LORD is about to pass by."

Then a great and powerful wind tore the mountains apart and shattered the rocks before the LORD, but the LORD was not in the wind. After the wind there was an earthquake, but the LORD was not in the earthquake. ¹²After the earth-quake came a fire, but the LORD was not in the fire. And after the fire came a gentle whisper. ¹³When Elijah heard it, he pulled his cloak over his face and went out and stood at the mouth of the cave.

Then a voice said to him, "What are you doing here, Elijah?"

¹⁴He replied, "I have been very zealous for the Lord God Almighty. The Israelites have rejected Your covenant, bro-ken down Your altars, and put Your prophets to death with the sword. I am the only one left, and now they are trying to kill me too."

¹⁵The LORD said to him, "Go back the way you came, and go to the Desert of Damascus. When you get there, anoint Hazael king over Aram. ¹⁶Also, anoint Jehu son of Nimshi king over Israel, and anoint Elisha son of Shaphat from Abel Meholah to succeed you as prophet. ¹⁷Jehu will put to death any who escape the sword of Hazael, and Elisha will put to death any who escape the sword of Jehu. ¹⁸Yet I reserve seven thousand in Israel—all whose knees have not bowed down to Baal and all whose mouths have not kissed him."

¹⁹So Elijah went from there and found Elisha son of Shaphat. He was plowing with twelve yoke of oxen, and he himself was driving the twelfth pair. Elijah went up to him and threw his cloak around him. ²⁰Elisha then left his oxen and ran after Elijah. "Let me kiss my father and mother good-by," he said, "and then I will come with you."

"Go back," Elijah replied. "What have I done to you?"

²¹So Elisha left him and went back. He took his yoke of oxen and slaughtered them. He burned the plowing equipment to cook the meat and gave it to the people, and they ate. Then he set out to follow Elijah and became his attendant.

1 Kings 19:1-21

When we look at the story of Elijah, we can be sure that God uses times of discouragement in our lives. God hasn't promised that our lives will be free from discouragement, but that He will help us cope during the discouraging times.

Let's look at what caused Elijah's discouragement. Look at the following passages and describe some of the things that caused Elijah to become discouraged.

1 Kings 19:1-2

1 Kings 19:3-5

1 Kings 19:8-10

Notice that it wasn't one particular thing that made Elijah discouraged, but several things. Elijah had just been through a tremendous experience where God worked through him and yet, just a few days later, he was depressed and despondent. God didn't leave him in discouragement, however. In His grace, the Lord prepared to lift Elijah up from the pits.

God provided specific means for Elijah to be encouraged. According to the following verses, what did He do to help Elijah through this period of discouragement?

1 Kings 19:5-7

1 Kings 19:9-10

46

1 Kings 19:11-13

1 Kings 19:14-18

1 Kings 19:19-21

 GROWING BY DOING

Attacking The Dragon

There were several things that seemed to add to Elijah's discouragement. Which of these can you most identify with when you become discouraged?

What triggers discouragement in you?

Which of God's antidotes for discouragement could help you get through discouraging times?

When you look at your life right now, would you say that there is a discouraging aspect to it? What is that aspect, and why is it discouraging to you?

What can you share with other group members this week that would lead them to encourage you in the midst of your situation?

GOING THE SECOND MILE

Thinking About Your Group
Undoubtedly, some people came to this group session with feelings of discouragement. As we learned in 1 Kings 19:19-21, God provides people to help in times of discouragement.

How can you be a help to someone in your group in order that they might not be discouraged?

What can you do for him or her? What will you plan on doing in the coming week?

Thinking About Yourself
Which of the following antidotes for discouragement do you need to be particularly aware of this week?

❑ Proper rest and diet?

❑ Honesty with God?

❑ Listening to the Word of God?

❑ Discovering you are not alone?

❑ Realizing that God has linked you up with someone else to help share the burden?

48

Thinking About Your World
Perhaps there is someone who is not in your small group, who is discouraged right now. How can you be an encourager to that person? What will you do to help that person?

FIVE

Lifted Up From Hopelessness

GroupSpeak: *"No matter how hard I try, my relationship with my son just deteriorates. I am at my wits end. I don't think it will ever get better. What troubles me most is that he seems to be straying from God."*

The Dragon of Hopelessness

Hope is a word that should be used often in a Christian's vocabulary. However, what our society calls "hope" is often very different from the description of hope found in the Scriptures.

The believer's future hope is as sure as Christ's resurrection from the dead. But many times the dragon of hopelessness attacks and renders us powerless. Hope is absolute certainty about the future, yet many of us draw back from speaking of a sure and certain hope because we think of hope as wishful thinking. So we wander around in helpless hopelessness. In this session, we will look at the topic of hopelessness in order to gain a vision of hope to restore our lives to wholeness.

GETTING ACQUAINTED

I Wish . . .

Think about some things you would like to do in the next six months. Is there a trip that you would like to go on or a project that you would like to tackle? Or perhaps there is something you wish you could acquire? Write down three things that would be at the top of your wish list.

1.

2.

3.

Are any of these hopes or wishes actually attainable?

What would you need to do in order to make these wishes a reality?

Share your wishes with the group and jot down one wish that someone else suggests that sounds particularly appealing to you.

 ## GAINING INSIGHT

Scripture Study

Paul was profoundly impacted by his understanding of the New Covenant—a covenant where people might respond to God not on the basis of demands, rules, and regulations, but on the basis of God's grace, received through faith in Christ. He knew this covenant would bring forth a new lifestyle characterized by the indwelling of the Holy Spirit. As you read 2 Corinthians 4:7-18, notice that Paul shows us how to live lives characterized by the hope of the Gospel, rather than by the hopelessness that characterizes so much of our world.

⁷But we have this treasure in jars of clay to show that this all-surpassing power is from God and not from us. ⁸We are hard pressed on every side, but not crushed; perplexed,

but not in despair; ⁹persecuted, but not abandoned; struck down, but not destroyed. ¹⁰We always carry around in our body the death of Jesus, so that the life of Jesus may also be revealed in our body. ¹¹For we who are alive are always being given over to death for Jesus' sake, so that His life may be revealed in our mortal body. ¹²So then, death is at work in us, but life is at work in you.

¹³It is written: "I believed; therefore I have spoken." With that same spirit of faith we also believe and therefore speak, ¹⁴because we know that the one who raised the Lord Jesus from the dead will also raise us with Jesus and present us with you in His presence. ¹⁵All this is for your benefit, so that the grace that is reaching more and more people may cause thanksgiving to overflow to the glory of God.

¹⁶Therefore we do not lose heart. Though outwardly we are being renewed day by day. ¹⁷For our light and momentary troubles are achieving for us an eternal glory that far outweighs them all. ¹⁸So we fix our eyes not on what is seen, but on what is unseen. For what is seen is temporary, but what is unseen is eternal.

2 Corinthians 4:7-18

In 2 Corinthians, Paul talked about his purpose in life and the ministry he had through God's Gospel. How could having meaning and purpose in life combat hopelessness?

How do you know that Paul knew what it was like to encounter great difficulties as he worked and ministered to other people?

How did Paul qualify his list of experiences in verses 8-9 to indicate what had not happened as a result of encountering difficulties?

Rephrase the principle found in verses 10-11 that describes how we might be able to see limitations or difficulties as positive times in our lives.

What specifically was Paul's hope as mentioned in verses 13-14?

According to verse 16, this hope should lead us to what experience or attitude? In what way do our present circumstances make this a difficult attitude to have?

According to verse 18, how can we make this attitude a definite part of our lives?

GROWING BY DOING

Attacking The Dragon

When we read about Paul's difficulties, did any situations come to mind where you had experienced those same difficulties?

❑ Hard pressed on every side

❑ Perplexed

❑ Persecuted

❑ Struck down

54

How has your faith affected the way you look at each of these circumstances?

In the midst of difficulties, we often feel confused and concerned. But Paul exhorts us to look beyond these things and fix our eyes on Jesus, on what is unseen, on those things that are eternal. How can you apply Paul's advice to your own life as you face momentary trials?

GOING THE SECOND MILE

Thinking About Your Group

One of the great ways of dealing with hopelessness is to have an eternal perspective. What kinds of songs or verses of Scripture could you share with other group members to point us to the unseen, the eternal?

What is special about these songs or verses that will have a strengthening effect on our hope?

Thinking About Yourself

Take another look at the list of difficulties you are perplexed or concerned about. What will you be doing in this coming week to gain an eternal perspective on these difficulties?

Thinking About Your World

Our world is plagued by feelings of hopelessness and despair. How can you gain perspective on global difficulties, political issues, economic problems, or specific situations that confront your own city or town?

SIX

From Doubt to Conviction

GroupSpeak: *"I would witness more, but I have some burning questions of my own."*

The Dragon of Doubt

Few people follow men and women of doubt. It's the people with tremendous conviction who attract crowds.

Dr. Martin Luther King was able to amass great numbers of people to follow him in his quest for racial equality because he was absolutely convinced of the justice of his position. This man of great conviction was able to reverse a trend of racial injustice and inequality. And while we still live with many civil rights problems, few would deny that King was a man of conviction.

Many years before him, William Wilberforce had a similar conviction that slavery was wrong. Wilberforce fought with tenacity in the British Parliament to end the scourge of incarcerating black Africans for profit. It was his conviction that led first to derision among his colleagues, but then to honor when he finally won the parliamentary vote.

Conviction leads to power. In the Christian life, conviction is extremely important, and yet many of us experience the shifting sands of doubt. In this session, we will attack the dragon of doubt that gnaws at the foundation of our lives.

GETTING ACQUAINTED

Shadows of Doubts

Tomorrow you will likely be faced with many situations that will go exactly as you have planned. What do you expect to happen tomorrow beyond a shadow of a doubt?

What are those things that are only probable events, that carry a certain measure of doubt?

What difference does a reliable car make in setting your schedule? How does a reliable alarm clock aid your sleep?

What does this tell you about the difference between doubt and conviction?

In what ways do doubts lead us to fear the future?

How do uncertainties in today's world lead to tentative living rather than to convicted living?

GAINING INSIGHT

Scripture Study
Read the following passages.

³⁶While they were still talking about this, Jesus Himself stood among them and said to them, "Peace be with you."

³⁷They were startled and frightened, thinking they saw a ghost. ³⁸He said to them, "Why are you troubled, and why do doubts rise in your minds? ³⁹Look at My hands and My feet. It is I Myself! Touch Me and see; a ghost does not have flesh and bones, as you see I have."

⁴⁰When He had said this, He showed them His hands and feet. ⁴¹And while they still did not believe it because of joy and amazement, He asked them, "Do you have anything here to eat?" ⁴²They gave Him a piece of broiled fish, ⁴³and He took it and ate it in their presence.

⁴⁴He said to them, "This is what I told you while I was still with you: Everything must be fulfilled that is written about Me in the Law of Moses, the Prophets and the Psalms."

⁴⁵Then He opened their minds so they could understand the Scriptures. ⁴⁶He told them, "This is what is written: The Christ will suffer and rise from the dead on the third day, ⁴⁷and repentance and forgiveness of sins will be preached in His name to all nations, beginning at Jerusalem. ⁴⁸You are witnesses of these things. ⁴⁹I am going to send you what My Father has promised; but stay in the city until you have been clothed with power from on high."

Luke 24:36-49

¹⁹On the evening of that first day of the week, when the disciples were together, with the doors locked for fear of the Jews, Jesus came and stood among them and said, "Peace be with you!" ²⁰After He said this, He showed them His hands and side. The disciples were overjoyed when they saw the Lord.

²¹Again Jesus said, "Peace be with you! As the Father has sent Me, I am sending you." ²²And with that He breathed

61

on them and said, "Receive the Holy Spirit. ²³If you forgive anyone his sins, they are forgiven; if you do not forgive them, they are not forgiven."

²⁴Now Thomas (called Didymus), one of the Twelve, was not with the disciples when Jesus came. ²⁵So the other disciples told him, "We have seen the Lord!"

But he said to them, "Unless I see the nail marks in His hands and put my finger where the nails were, and put my hand into His side, I will not believe it."

²⁶A week later His disciples were in the house again, and Thomas was with them. Though the doors were locked, Jesus came and stood among them and said, "Peace be with you!" ²⁷Then He said to Thomas, "Put your finger here; see My hands. Reach out your hand and put it into My side. Stop doubting and believe."

²⁸Thomas said to Him, "My Lord and my God!"

²⁹Then Jesus told him, "Because you have seen Me, you have believed; blessed are those who have not seen and yet have believed."

³⁰Jesus did many other miraculous signs in the presence of His disciples, which are not recorded in this book. ³¹But these are written that you may believe that Jesus is the Christ, the Son of God, and that by believing you may have life in His name.

John 20:19-31

In the Scriptures we find a tremendous difference between people with conviction and people with doubt. In fact, in these two passages, we find that the same people act in very different ways depending on whether they're filled with conviction or doubt.

Based on Luke 24:37-42, what evidence did Jesus give of His resurrection?

In Luke 24:36, Jesus said, "Peace be with you." How does certainty of Christ's resurrection lead us to peace?

What are things that we face in the future that require a life full of conviction rather than doubt?

How do these facts concerning Christ's resurrection help us when we are given the command to be Christ's witnesses?

Jesus promised that we might receive power through the Holy Spirit. How does this help in our proclamation of the Gospel to other people?

What do you know about the Book of Acts that would indicate that the disciples changed from doubt to conviction regarding their understanding of Jesus after His death?

In John 20:19 how would you characterize the attitude and behavior of the disciples? What prompted this?

Compare the disciples' response to Jesus' sudden appearance in John 20:19-20 with their response in Luke 24:37, 41.

We frequently think that Thomas (often called "doubting Thomas") had a tremendous lack of faith. But would we be any different? How did Jesus answer Thomas' doubt in John 20:26-27?

What was Thomas' response to Jesus' actions?

Jesus apparently had us in mind when He said, "Blessed are those who have not seen and yet have believed" (John 20:29). How does Jesus' response to Thomas help us live lives of conviction?

According to John 20:31, why did God give us these evidences of Christ's miraculous power and His resurrection?

 GROWING BY DOING

Attacking The Dragon
Put yourself in the disciples' sandals. Prior to His post-resurrection appearances, would you have believed Christ's prediction about His resurrection? In other words, would you have been a "Thomas" or would you have simply believed in the words of Jesus?

What makes it difficult to believe in the Resurrection?

How can we encourage one another in the truths of these Scriptures in order to be effective witnesses for Christ?

How will you change the way you share your faith with others to an action that naturally flows from your conviction?

Write a prayer of thanks to God for certainty about who Jesus is and how this certainty will affect your life.

Dear God,

GOING THE SECOND MILE

Thinking About Your Group
Is there a verse that has particularly struck you as providing the conviction that you need in your life? Try sharing it with someone in the group during this week.

Thinking About Yourself
Write down one situation that you face that will become easier to face if you approach it with the conviction of knowing who Christ is and with the power that Jesus has given to us as a result of His resurrection.

How will you determine to give this situation to the Lord and live in the light of His promises?

Thinking About Your World
One of the chief concerns that Jesus had at the end of the Gospel of Luke was to prepare the disciples as His witnesses for the world. Your world may not encompass huge lands and countries, but undoubtedly there are people in your sphere of influence who need exposure to your witness. Who are these people and how can you be effective in sharing your convictions with them?

SEVEN

Shedding Bitterness

GroupSpeak: *"I just can't forget what happened. There is no way I will speak to him again!"*

The Dragon of Bitterness

It's not unusual to feel angry. In fact, Paul told the Ephesians it was OK to be angry, but that they shouldn't let the sun go down on their anger and give Satan a foothold in their lives (Ephesians 4:26-27).

Paul knew that if anger goes unchecked, it will result in bitterness. The same result is produced by unchecked disappointment.

If anyone had an opportunity to be disappointed and bitter, it was Joseph. But, in spite of the disappointments and injustices he experienced, Joseph saw a higher purpose for what God had in store. He channeled his disappointment in such a way that bitterness did not follow.

Have you ever known a person whose life was filled with the stench of bitterness? These people are not much fun to be around as they attack those who disappoint them. It's probably safe to assume that at some point in our lives, we all have experienced disappointments, injustices, and problems with people that have led to resentment and bitterness.

Bitterness drains the life out of personal relationships. When disappointment, jealousy, or sin cause a breach between two people, there's always a danger that those same people will choose to respond in bitterness rather than in reconciliation and restoration. The story of Joseph in Genesis 37–45 portrays how broken relationships led to bitterness and how Joseph overcame this dragon.

GETTING ACQUAINTED

Significant Relationships
Describe one very meaningful relationship that you have had in your life. What was that relationship built upon?

Why was it a successful relationship?

What relationship right now are you hoping to nurture?

What are the barriers in nurturing that relationship?

GAINING INSIGHT

Scripture Study
Read the following episodes that marked Joseph's life.

³Now Israel loved Joseph more than any of his other sons, because he had been born to him in his old age; and he made a richly ornamented robe for him. ⁴When his broth-

70

ers saw that their father loved him more than any of them, they hated him and could not speak a kind word to him. . . .

¹⁹"Here comes that dreamer!" they said to each other. ²⁰"Come now, let's kill him and throw him into one of these cisterns and say that a ferocious animal devoured him. Then we'll see what comes of his dreams."

²¹When Reuben heard this, he tried to rescue him from their hands. "Let's not take his life," he said. ²²"Don't shed any blood. Throw him into this cistern here in the desert, but don't lay a hand on him." Reuben said this to rescue him from them and take him back to his father.

²³So when Joseph came to his brothers, they stripped him of his robe—the richly ornamented robe he was wearing—²⁴and they took him and threw him into the cistern. Now the cistern was empty; there was no water in it.

Genesis 37:3-4, 19-24

Why do you think Joseph's brothers were moved to take such drastic action against him?

What do you think marked their relationship with Joseph?

How did they handle their own disappointments and jealousies?

What steps do you think were taken that allowed bitterness to take such deep root in Joseph's brothers?

Now read this passage for more insight into Joseph's life.

¹Now Joseph had been taken down to Egypt. Potiphar, an Egyptian who was one of Pharaoh's officials, the captain of the guard, bought him from the Ishmaelites who had taken him there.

²The LORD was with Joseph and he prospered, and he lived in the house of his Egyptian master. ³When his master saw that the LORD was with him and that the LORD gave him success in everything he did, ⁴Joseph found favor in his eyes and became his attendant. Potiphar put him in charge of his household, and he entrusted to his care everything he owned. ⁵From the time he put him in charge of his household and of all that he owned, the LORD blessed the household of the Egyptian because of Joseph. The blessing of the LORD was on everything Potiphar had, both in the house and in the field. ⁶So he left in Joseph's care everything he had; with Joseph in charge, he did not concern himself with anything except the food he ate.

Now Joseph was well-built and handsome.

Genesis 39:1-6

After Joseph was sold into slavery, he was placed into service by a high-placed official within the court of Pharaoh. How did Joseph handle this very disappointing situation, having gone from being the prized son of his father's house to being a slave? What seemed to mark his behavior?

Joseph was accused of rape by Potiphar's wife. Keep in mind what Joseph must have been feeling as you read about how he was treated by his master.

¹⁹When his master heard the story his wife told him, saying, "This is how your slave treated me," he burned with anger. ²⁰Joseph's master took him and put him in prison, the place where the king's prisoners were confined.

But while Joseph was there in the prison, ²¹the LORD was with him; He showed him kindness and granted him favor in the eyes of the prison warden. ²²So the warden put Joseph in charge of all those held in the prison, and he was made responsible for all that was done there. ²³The warden paid no attention to anything under Joseph's care, because the LORD was with Joseph and gave him success in whatever he did.

Genesis 39:19-23

After Joseph was falsely accused of the attempted rape of the master's wife, he was thrown into prison. How do you think Joseph reacted to this new situation in prison?

Besides being a wonderful manager, Joseph also had the ability to interpret dreams. Yet he had to endure another disappointment after he gave a precise interpretation of the dreams of a cupbearer and a baker being held in prison.

The cupbearer was restored to his previous position and the baker was killed, just as Joseph had predicted. Yet according to Genesis 40:23, the chief cupbearer forgot about Joseph's prediction. Imagine how Joseph must have felt. Nevertheless, he was able to interpret a dream for Pharaoh two years after interpreting the dream for the chief cupbearer.

¹⁵Pharaoh said to Joseph, "I had a dream, and no one can interpret it. But I have heard it said of you that when you hear a dream you can interpret it."

¹⁶"I cannot do it," Joseph replied to Pharaoh, "but God will give Pharaoh the answer he desires."

¹⁷Then Pharaoh said to Joseph, "In my dream I was standing on the bank of the Nile, ¹⁸when out of the river there came up seven cows, fat and sleek, and they grazed among the reeds. ¹⁹After them, seven other cows came up—scrawny and very ugly and lean. I had never seen

such ugly cows in all the land of Egypt. ²⁰The lean, ugly cows ate up the seven fat cows that came up first. ²¹But even after they ate them, no one could tell that they had done so; they looked just as ugly as before. Then I woke up.

²²"In my dreams I also saw seven heads of grain, full and good, growing on a single stalk. ²³After them, seven other heads sprouted—withered and thin and scorched by the east wind. ²⁴The thin heads of grain swallowed up the seven good heads. I told this to the magicians, but none could explain it to me." . . .

³⁹Then Pharaoh said to Joseph, "Since God has made all this known to you, there is no one so discerning and wise as you. ⁴⁰You shall be in charge of my palace, and all my people are to submit to your orders. Only with respect to the throne will I be greater than you."

⁴¹"So Pharaoh said to Joseph, "I hereby put you in charge of the whole land of Egypt." ⁴²Then Pharaoh took his signet ring from his finger and put it on Joseph's finger. He dressed him in robes of fine linen and put a gold chain around his neck. ⁴³He had him ride in a chariot as his second-in-command, and men shouted before him, "Make way!" Thus he put him in charge of the whole land of Egypt.

Genesis 41:15-24, 39-43

After all his bad experiences, how do you think Joseph felt about Pharaoh's decision to put him in charge of Egypt?

Eventually Joseph was reunited with his brothers who had sold him into slavery. Certainly this would have been a fearful day for his brothers, and yet at the time when Joseph finally revealed himself to them, notice how Joseph responded to these men.

³Joseph said to his brothers, "I am Joseph! Is my father still living?" But his brothers were not able to answer him, because they were terrified at his presence.

⁴Then Joseph said to his brothers, "Come close to me." When they had done so, he said, "I am your brother Joseph, the one you sold into Egypt! ⁵And now, do not be distressed and do not be angry with yourselves for selling me here, because it was to save lives that God sent me ahead of you. ⁶For two years now there has been famine in the land, and for the next five years there will not be plowing and reaping. ⁷But God sent me ahead of you to preserve for you a remnant on earth and to save your lives by a great deliverance.

⁸"So then, it was not you who sent me here, but God. He made me father to Pharaoh, lord of his entire household and ruler of all Egypt."

Genesis 45:3-8

What do you think made the difference between the way Joseph responded to the difficult circumstances that resulted from his broken relationship with his brothers and the way the brothers responded to Joseph?

Regardless of whether we think young Joseph was prudent in the way he spoke to his brothers or in his boasts about how he would rule over them, we must be impressed with how he handled difficult circumstances that could have left him filled with bitterness.

Joseph's experience speaks to many of us who go through grave disappointments and bitterness. How would you summarize Joseph's strategy for handling bitterness?

GROWING BY DOING

Attacking The Dragon

Do you have any disappointments that seem to be staring you in the face at this point? What are they?

If you could rank those disappointments on a scale of 1–10, with 1 being a minor disappointment and 10 being a major disappointment, how would you rank these different disappointments?

Do any of your relationships need healing? What is that relationship and how can you take steps to relieve the bitterness that rests there?

How might you gain a tremendous sense of confidence in what God can do in the midst of disappointing times?

Which of these areas of disappointment could you share with the group in order to gain their prayer support for you?

GOING THE SECOND MILE

Thinking About Your Group

Have we been disappointed by our small group? Perhaps this week is a good time to discuss where our group is at and to express a sense of satisfaction or dissatisfaction about the way the group is operating. This can be a time of evaluation, to talk about whether or not our group is meeting interpersonal needs, worshiping as we ought, supporting one another.

How could such evaluation cause us to be freed from bitterness?

Thinking About Yourself

Disappointments are normal in our lives; we would like to totally eradicate them. But such disappointments will be with us until we are united with Christ in heaven. Can you form a battle plan in order to relinquish some of the resentment and bitterness that may have crept in because of unrealized potential or a dissatisfaction about the direction of your life? Will you be able to commit yourself to be faithful even though extremely disappointed?

During times of disappointment, resentment, and discouragement, it is good to pause and reflect on those things that are going well, that God has allowed us to experience that are positive. What are some of those positive things? Write a prayer of thanksgiving for the good things and an appeal to God for those things that are less than satisfying.

Dear God,

Thinking About Your World
Who around you do you think is experiencing a deep sense of need and dissatisfaction about his or her circumstances?

How can you make contact with this person or family in order to bring a word of comfort and admonishment to remain faithful to what God has called them to do? Write this person's name down and what steps you will take to make this kind of admonishment and expression of comfort a reality.

78

EIGHT

Handling Failure

GroupSpeak: *"I've tried that before and it doesn't work. You can't imagine how hard it is to look in the mirror after another failure in my life."*

The Dragon of Failure

There is no question about it—failure is one of the most difficult experiences for humans. Nobody wants to receive a consolation prize at a tournament when they were competing for the championship trophy. It doesn't satisfy the fans to know that their team is second best, or third best. They want to know that their team is a winner.

And while there may be some sports figures and sports teams that have an incredible ability to win, at some point they usually experience failure and disappointment. In baseball, for instance, if a batter fails to get a hit 7 out of 10 times at the plate, he is considered to be a hero, not a failure. To hit .300 is outstanding in professional baseball.

Most of us at times fall short of either others' expectations, our expectations, or perhaps even God's commands. In this session, we will take a look at how we can handle failure.

GETTING ACQUAINTED

What I Do Best

What is it that you really do well? What kind of a skill, sport, or procedure have you excelled at?

What is it about that task that makes it easy for you, or why do you enjoy it so much? (assuming that you do)

What kind of a skill or sport are you very poor at?

What is the difference in the way you approach each of those tasks? How do you feel when you are successful in what you are trying to accomplish? When you fail?

GAINING INSIGHT

Scripture Study

One of the primary strategies for handling failure is to sense the tremendous love of God in the midst of failure. We will look at this strategy as we see how Peter related to Jesus before and after His crucifixion.

⁵⁴Then seizing Him, they led Him away and took Him into the house of the high priest. Peter followed at a distance. ⁵⁵But when they had kindled a fire in the middle of the courtyard and had sat down together, Peter sat down with

them. ⁵⁶A servant girl saw him seated there in the firelight. She looked closely at him and said, "This man was with Him."

⁵⁷But he denied it. "Woman, I don't know Him," he said.

⁵⁸A little later someone else saw him and said, "You also are one of them."

"Man, I am not!" Peter replied.

⁵⁹About an hour later another asserted, "Certainly this fellow was with Him, for he is a Galilean."

⁶⁰Peter replied, "Man, I don't know what you're talking about!" Just as he was speaking, the rooster crowed. ⁶¹The Lord turned and looked straight at Peter. Then Peter remembered the word the Lord had spoken to him: "Before the rooster crows today, you will disown Me three times." ⁶²And he went outside and wept bitterly.

Luke 22:54-62

After these events, Peter abandoned Jesus. Jesus was crucified and placed in the tomb. Peter had failed miserably in his role as a follower of Jesus. Though the post-Crucifixion appearances of Christ to the disciples totally changed Peter's outlook, we can be sure that Peter's bitter failure was vividly in his mind. As the following account indicates, Jesus dealt gently with His disciple.

¹⁵When they had finished eating, Jesus said to Simon Peter, "Simon son of John, do you truly love Me more than these?"

"Yes, Lord," he said, "You know that I love You."

Jesus said, "Feed My lambs."

¹⁶Again Jesus said, "Simon son of John, do you truly love Me?"

He answered, "Yes, Lord, You know that I love You."

83

Jesus said, "Take care of My sheep."

¹⁷The third time He said to him, "Simon son of John, do you love Me?"

Peter was hurt because Jesus asked him the third time, "Do you love Me?" He said, "Lord, You know all things; You know that I love You."

Jesus said, "Feed My sheep. ¹⁸I tell you the truth, when you were younger you dressed yourself and went where you wanted; but when you are old you will stretch out your hands, and someone else will dress you and lead you where you do not want to go." ¹⁹Jesus said this to indicate the kind of death by which Peter would glorify God. Then He said to him, "Follow Me!"

²⁰Peter turned and saw that the disciple whom Jesus loved was following them. (This was the one who had leaned back against Jesus at the supper and had said, "Lord, who is going to betray You?") ²¹When Peter saw him, he asked, "Lord, what about him?"

²²Jesus answered, "If I want him to remain alive until I return, what is that to you? You must follow Me."

John 21:15-22

When we look at the story of the denial and reinstatement of Peter, we get the impression that Peter had terribly disappointed Jesus. Though Jesus had predicted his failure, that probably did not lessen the pain of that failure for Jesus or Peter.

Describe the pressures that Peter might have felt when he was questioned about Jesus in Luke 22:54-62. What was the tone of Peter's responses?

How did Peter respond when he rejected Jesus for the third time and heard the rooster crow?

In John 21:15-22 we find that Jesus graciously reached out to Peter in a way that restored Peter's position and assured him of Jesus' love. Why do you think that Jesus questioned Peter's love at this point?

How do you think Peter felt about Jesus' questions?

What is significant about the number of times that Jesus questioned Peter's love?

Why did Peter question Jesus about John? What was Jesus' response?

What does this say about comparing both the performance and position of children of God?

GROWING BY DOING

Attacking The Dragon
How should we handle those times when we disappoint ourselves, others, or even God?

What are those things we can keep in mind using Peter's experience with Jesus as a model?

What is the hardest part about failing? Is it the fact that we didn't accomplish what we set out to do? Is it that we'll have to try again? Is it the feeling of not being adequate, or is it the realization that we may have disappointed others?

Think about a time when you felt like you had really failed someone. How could you move beyond those feelings of insecurity or inferiority to get to an assurance that you are a restored person?

Read 1 John 1:9-10.

⁹If we confess our sins, He is faithful and just and will forgive us our sins and purify us from all unrighteousness. ¹⁰If we claim we have not sinned, we make Him out to be a liar and His word has no place in our lives.

1 John 1:9-10

If you have failed God, how can you be sure that you have a restored position with Him?

There is another way that we can help in times of failure—we can deal with one another in a way that is gracious and affirming. Can you think of anyone who has failed you? How can you be more like Jesus in the way you affirm that person?

GOING THE SECOND MILE

Thinking About Your Group

In what way can you affirm the talents and gifts of your group members?

What steps can you take this week to give that affirmation?

Thinking About Yourself

In what way have you either been a failure recently or have experienced the failure of another person in your life? How will you attack this particular assault of the dragon?

Thinking About Your World

No one likes to be criticized. And people who have a good word for others often are very well liked. Our world is full of failures and we can pave the way for the Gospel in many people's lives if they see us as being safe and affirming.

Is there someone in your life you can affirm in the job he or she is doing—even though he or she may have disappointed you at some time or another? How and when will you do this?

DEAR SMALL GROUP LEADER:

Picture Yourself As A Leader.

List some words that describe what would excite you or scare you as a leader of your small group.

A Leader Is Not . . .
- ☐ a person with all the answers.
- ☐ responsible for everyone having a good time.
- ☐ someone who does all the talking.
- ☐ likely to do everything perfectly.

A Leader Is . . .
- ☐ someone who encourages and enables group members to discover insights and build relationships.
- ☐ a person who helps others meet their goals, enabling the group to fulfill its purpose.
- ☐ a protector to keep members from being attacked or taken advantage of.
- ☐ the person who structures group time and plans ahead.
- ☐ the facilitator who stimulates relationships and participation by asking questions.

❑ an affirmer, encourager, challenger.
❑ enthusiastic about the small group, about God's Word, and about discovering and growing.

What Is Important To Small Group Members?
❑ A leader who cares about them.
❑ Building relationships with other members.
❑ Seeing themselves grow.
❑ Belonging and having a place in the group.
❑ Feeling safe while being challenged.
❑ Having their reasons for joining a group fulfilled.

What Do You Do . . .

If nobody talks—
❑ Wait—show the group members you expect them to answer.
❑ Rephrase a question—give them time to think.
❑ Divide into subgroups so all participate.

If somebody talks too much—
❑ Avoid eye contact with him or her.
❑ Sit beside the person next time. It will be harder for him or her to talk sitting by the leader.
❑ Suggest, "Let's hear from someone else."
❑ Interrupt with, "Great! Anybody else?"

If people don't know the Bible—
❑ Print out the passage in the same translation and hand it out to save time searching for a passage.
❑ Use the same Bible versions and give page numbers.
❑ Ask enablers to sit next to those who may need encouragement in sharing.
❑ Begin using this book to teach them how to study; affirm their efforts.

If you have a difficult individual—
❑ Take control to protect the group, but recognize that exploring differences can be a learning experience.
❑ Sit next to that person.
❑ To avoid getting sidetracked or to protect another group member, you may need to interrupt, saying, "Not all of us feel that way."
❑ Pray for that person before the group meeting.

ONE

Winning Over Worry

"Do not be anxious about anything," the Apostle Paul said in Philippians 4:6. We may complain, saying, "But, Paul, you don't know my situation!" Yet our plight cannot be any worse than his—possible death by execution.

Even in the midst of imprisonment, Paul could see good coming from it. He recognized that what happened to him, though unpleasant, actually served to advance the Gospel (Philippians 1:12-14). Through life or death, Paul knew he would be delivered by Christ (Philippians 1:19-21).

Most of us do not go around the world establishing churches as Paul did. Instead of such excitement and a pioneering lifestyle, we lead fairly normal lives. Nonetheless, anxiety seems to plague us and our society. We worry about our health, our jobs, our financial situations, our family, our reputations. We could even worry about how much anxiety we have!

God's way, however, is the road to contentment. The Holy Spirit inspired the Apostle Paul to give guidelines for attaining this elusive quality. Gaining contentment leads to freedom. Through Jesus Christ, we can put to death (or at least mortally wound) that dragon called anxiety.

As **Group Leader** of this small group experience, *you* have a choice as to which elements will best fit your group, your style of leadership, and your purposes. After you examine the **Session Objectives**, select the activities under each heading with which to begin your community building. You have many choices.

SESSION OBJECTIVES

√ To get acquainted by sharing the events which make up our day-to-day lives.

√ To listen as others open up their lives to the group.

√ To learn from Paul how to combat worry and anxiety.

√ To remember the items for which we can truly rejoice.

√ To decide how to attack anxiety and worry in our own lives.

√ To be equipped to encourage others on how to handle anxiety.

GETTING ACQUAINTED   20–30 minutes

Pocket Principle

1 A small group is always more effective if its members are closely knit through the sharing of experiences, needs, attitudes, and resources. Having an opening question which relates to the material studied but does not require a lot of preparation helps create community. The question should be nonthreatening and able to be answered by all. This is not classified as "surface talk" since people are learning things about each other.

If your group is not well acquainted, take time at least to get to know one another's names before beginning this session.

If the group is strong in its relational bonds, the following exercises may help to strengthen the group.

Have a group member read aloud **The Dragon of Worry**. Then choose one of the following activities to help create a more comfortable, nonthreatening atmosphere for the first meeting of your small group.

A Snapshot of Your Day

The more we understand about one another, the more effective we will be in applying Scripture to our lives and encouraging others to learn and apply the Scriptures to their own lives. As a result of these opening questions, we will find that group members indeed are being bonded to one another.

In this snapshot of your day, try to give group members an opportunity to talk about themselves and listen to the events of others' days. You will notice that one question that isn't asked is: "What do you do for a living?" This question is loaded with difficulties as it often implies class distinctions and roles.

After each person shares what their day was like, discuss the questions. Don't expect to answer all the questions, but allow group members to choose which questions they will answer.

Notice that part of this section includes a discussion about anxiety or worry. This is to enable us to focus on the topic for this session. The most important questions are:

❑ **How do you know when concerns progress to anxiety or worry?**
❑ **What are the reasons for our worry and anxiety today?**

Encourage group members to add appropriate items to their Worry Lists as they focus more specifically on those items that are of concern. Note that we will return to this List at the end of the study in order for group members to apply Paul's principles for combating anxiety and worry.

Discuss how the world adds to our discontent. There are many things that our society does that increases our worry. For example, the media urges us to buy things that we supposedly need, adding to our lack of contentment with what we have. Stories of violence in our cities add a certain level of discontent for our own well being and safety. In these ways, the world adds to our discontent.

At the end of this section, ask group members to keep their eyes open for any hints that may relieve anxiety or worry in Paul's letter to the Philippians.

Pocket Principle

2 A strong group leader asks a question and allows group members to have interaction with one another, not just with the leader. The group leader can model good communication in a small group through listening.

 GAINING INSIGHT   30–35 minutes

Scripture Study
Before reading Philippians 4:4-13 aloud, ask group members to listen carefully for principles that might help them deal with worry and anxiety. Ask volunteers to read the Scriptures, possibly separating the text into three sections or paragraphs:

❑ Section 1 (4:4-7)
❑ Section 2 (4:8-9)
❑ Section 3 (4:10-14)

Pocket Principle

3 We should never call on group members to read unless we are sure that: (1) they desire to read; (2) they feel as if they will not be put on the spot. Instead, ask for volunteers for such a role as reading the Scriptures. It may not be much to us to be called upon to read, but for some persons it can be a terrifying experience— one that may convince a person, particularly a newcomer, not to come back.

Point out that Paul was not sitting in a plush hotel when he wrote these words. He may have been facing execution for being a Christian. So when he talks of contentment and joy, he probably had little on an earthly scale to be joyful about. Yet his letter to the Philippians exudes joy which bubbles over with contentment. Though he may have had little opportunity to be content, his joy was abundant.

Discuss the following questions:

☐ **What terms are used today for the word rejoice?** (Because the word is not used very much in our culture, it is important to identify some synonyms to make appropriate connections. For example, some group members may suggest the terms "be happy" or "grateful." Again, the important thing is to get group members thinking along the lines of being able to get beyond circumstances and see what God can do in their lives that transcends their circumstances.)

☐ **In what ways does rejoicing diminish anxiety?** (It makes us feel better when we rejoice in the midst of worry and anxiety.)

☐ **How do we actually go about rejoicing?** (We can verbally thank God for what He is doing or sing songs of thankfulness.)

☐ **According to verses 6-7, what is another antidote to anxiety?** (Note that Paul includes prayer and petition but links the prayers and petitions with thanksgiving so that while we are presenting our requests to God, we are also presenting a thankful heart to God. We ought not to simply bring a wish list to the Heavenly Father, but we ought to bring forth attitudes that are ready to receive what God wills. We can bring a list of the things that we are concerned about, but we must seek the peace that God will certainly give regarding whatever transcends. In other words, we can have the peace of God in the midst of difficulty. What we need during anxious times is not an instant answer to what we perceive our needs are, but the joy and peace of God.)

❑ **Why are verses 6-7 so difficult to practice?** (Try to get a glimpse into the way group members respond to an admonition to pray with thanksgiving. There may be several different attitudes that people would have about prayer. One person may say that it is simply not worth it because he or she feels very far from God right now, that God wouldn't listen to him or her. Another person might say that he has prayed to God in the past but God didn't do what he asked.)

❑ **Notice Paul's attitude in verses 11-12. Summarize it in your own words.** (The attitude itself might be summarized in one word—*contentment*.)

❑ **How does verse 13 provide us with the ultimate answer to our anxieties?** (Paul urged the Philippian believers to learn the secret of contentment. Paul knew what it was like to be in desperate need, and yet [with his background] he also knew what it was like to have an abundance of material items as well as friends. How we could learn from Paul since we are surrounded daily by those who have not understood the secret of contentment!)

Discuss how this secret or mystery really is the ultimate answer for our anxieties. Certainly, we must endeavor to understand that Jesus is in ultimate control of the universe, and that even though we may undergo trials and extreme situations, God has not lost sight of us. He can show Himself strong even when we are at the weakest of points in our lives. In fact, this is what Paul learned as he struggled with his own inadequacies with his thorn in the flesh.

GROWING BY DOING   15–20 minutes

Attacking The Dragon
Have group members examine their Worry Lists and discuss the questions in this section.

Levels of Contentment
Ask group members to work on their own to rate their levels of contentment in the suggested areas. Then ask volunteers to share one area where they need to become more content.

Close in prayer, asking God to help each person find contentment in his or her specific area of concern.

GOING THE SECOND MILE   5–10 minutes

Challenge group members to complete this section on their own. Encourage them to pray for each other during the coming weeks. Ask them to spend some time thinking about how they can combat anxiety and share what they've learned about finding contentment with others.

GROWING AS A LEADER

Evaluation is both threatening and imperative. It is threatening because it points out inadequacies in ourselves. It is imperative because we have inadequacies! But self-evaluation is less threatening because the evaluator cares about oneself. Since this is the first session of this series, evaluate the interaction between group members during the **Getting Acquainted** part of the session.

❏ Did you allow enough time for group members to talk with each other?
❏ Did you dominate the conversation by always interjecting something?

TWO

Freedom From Fear

"Be strong and courageous," God said to Joshua as he inherited the leadership of the nation of Israel. Though God gave him this command, Joshua certainly had reason to fear. He was about to encounter a hostile enemy as he entered the Promised Land; he had to fill the sandals of a powerful, dynamic leader; and experience indicated that even Joshua's own people might be hostile toward his leadership or *any* leadership for that matter!

We may have difficulty identifying exactly with someone like Joshua. We don't go around conquering new lands and leading nations, but many of us encounter fearful situations regularly in our lives. As the world moves at a breakneck pace, we are challenged at every turn with new situations that often threaten our livelihood, our families, and our very lives. Yet God has not allowed us to live in the midst of fear without any empowering to overcome such a dragon.

As **Group Leader** of this small group experience, *you* have a choice as to which elements will best fit your group, your style of leadership, and your purposes. After you examine the **Session Objectives**, select the activities under each heading with which to begin your community building.

SESSION OBJECTIVES

√ To get acquainted by sharing some of the fears which may hound us.

√ To listen as others open up their lives to the group.

√ To learn from the example of how God interacted with Joshua to combat fear.

√ To recall God's promises and commands to help fight the dragon of fear.

√ To decide how to appropriate the gifts and promises God gives.

√ To be equipped to encourage others on how to overcome fearfulness.

GETTING ACQUAINTED   20–25 minutes

Have a group member read aloud **The Dragon of Fear.** Then choose one of the following activities to help create a more comfortable, nonthreatening atmosphere.

Fears And Phobias
Ask the group to disclose some of their fears. This may be threatening to some group members and, therefore, they should be allowed to *pass* on the questions in this activity. You will find that group members can pick one of the phobias to comment on at a "safe" distance. If the group seems too large, break it into smaller groups of three or four in order to facilitate more sharing. Sharing such experiences provides a helpful glimpse into individuals' backgrounds and may even help some to appreciate other members of the group more fully.

After discussing the questions, point out that most people don't talk about fear. Ask: **Is it because of embarrassment? Fear about talking about fear? Seeming to be weak? What do you think? How does our society deal with this issue?**

Pocket Principle

1 As Group Leader, you need to share some of your own fears to help group members seriously think about their own insecurities. When people see that you are open, they are much more likely to be open themselves.

Optional — Questions on Fear
If your group members seem reluctant to share some of their phobias, focus on the positive side of this issue — security. Ask these less threatening questions:

❑ **What was one time in your life when you felt very secure and free from fear?**
❑ **Why did you feel such security?**

GAINING INSIGHT   30–35 minutes

Scripture Study
Have group members read aloud Joshua 1:1-18. Split up the oral reading of the Scripture to keep interest and concentration. Discuss the specific commands given to Joshua:

❑ "get ready" (v. 2)
❑ "be strong and courageous" (vv. 6-7, 9, 18)
❑ "be careful to obey all the law" (v. 7)
❑ "do not turn from [the law]" (v. 7)
❑ "do not let the Book of the Law depart from your mouth" (v. 8)
❑ "meditate on it day and night" (v. 8)
❑ "do not be terrified" (v. 9)
❑ "do not be discouraged" (v. 9)

These are the commands given to Joshua as he prepared to lead the people. It would have been a very intimidating prospect to follow in Moses' shoes. But God did not leave Joshua without help.

It is not necessary for every person to find every command. It is probable that some will find commands others will miss. After you go over the commands, discuss the following questions:

100

❑ **Why do you think God had to remind Joshua to be strong and courageous? Was there anything that Joshua had to fear? What were the tasks that had to be done? What lay ahead of Joshua and his country-men?** (It is not hard to figure out why Joshua was admonished to "Be strong and courageous." He was on the eve of a battle to occupy a new homeland. It would not be an easy road ahead. In addition, the loyalty of the nation was to Moses, not to Joshua. As with any change of bosses, some will not accept a new leader. Joshua had reason to fear, but God was greater than the fear.

Point out that sometimes fear is reasonable. But the believer in Jesus can overcome that fear with the sure promises of God. Then discuss these questions:

❑ **First of all, what did God promise about His presence?** (God promised that He would be with Joshua forever, wherever he went. In the depths of fear and doubt, God was there for Joshua. Today, we have the presence of the Holy Spirit to give us comfort, challenge, and conviction of sin [John 7:34-39]. The Holy Spirit is the sign from God that we belong to Him. Refer to Matthew 28:19-20 where Jesus states that He will be with us "always, to the very end of the age." This should motivate us to action.)

❑ **Second, what did God promise to do for Joshua in verses 3-6?** (He promised to give Joshua land and assurance of victory over enemies. It was a promise of future action on the part of God.)

❑ **Third, what did God give Joshua to help him in his new role as chief of the Israelite army?** (He gave Joshua the Book of the Law for a resource.)

❑ **What does this Book of the Law in verse 8 represent for the believer? How can God alleviate some of our fears through the use of this resource?** (This Book, of course, is the Bible. God's promises and words of comfort can be a tremendous asset for alleviating fears.)

The people would have naturally been concerned with the death of their leader, and at such an inopportune time. But God knew what He was doing and would be able to lead the people to victory at the hands of Joshua. God is not bound by circumstances.

GROWING BY DOING   15–20 minutes

Attacking The Dragon

This is a very personal section, dealing with group members' fears and concerns. As such, it must be dealt with sensitively. Keep your ears open for prayer opportunities.

Pocket Principle

2 Many small group leaders wait until a certain time of the meeting to have prayer. This is neither necessary nor recommended for certain situations. If someone has shared something which is obviously very troubling, then pause right there to pray for that person.

Work for disclosure during this section. Ask group members to break into smaller groups of two or three. Notice that God gave Joshua the people of Israel to encourage him. So also God has given us each other, not for judgment, but to help one another. And so we must give group members that kind of opportunity to do just that!

GOING THE SECOND MILE   5–10 minutes

Challenge group members to complete this section on their own. Encourage them to pray for each other during the coming weeks. Ask them to spend some time thinking about how they can combat fear by drawing on God's presence, promises, and providence. Close by giving the small groups of two or three opportunity to pray for specific fears they are experiencing.

GROWING AS A LEADER

Examine your responsiveness to the various needs brought out by the members of the group. Did you lead the group to prayer when a heavy concern was shared with the group?

THREE

Overcoming Temptation

When thinking about the temptation of Jesus, we are prone to conclude that Jesus is God and, therefore, He is empowered specially with the ability not to sin.

The picture painted in the New Testament, however, is one where Jesus is a real human being who encountered real temptations and struggles with sin. He is victorious because He called upon the strength and ammunition from God to defeat the dragon of temptation.

In this session, we will discover what tools Jesus used in responding to temptation. Discussing temptation will require some general questioning as well as more specific probing of where people are at. The goal is to provide a time when people can discern what characterizes their lives regarding temptation and how to enhance their opportunities for victory in the midst of temptation.

As **Group Leader** of this small group experience, *you* have a choice as to which elements will best fit your group, your style of leadership, and your purposes. After you examine the **Session Objectives**, select the activities under each heading with which to begin your community building.

104

SESSION OBJECTIVES

√ To get acquainted by discussing the roles people play and by probing the possible temptations they may face because of those roles.

√ To listen as others open up their lives to the group.

√ To discover from the account of Jesus' life how we can handle temptation.

√ To discuss how to handle specific sin tendency areas.

√ To increase the sense of need for accountability and for the actual implementation of accountability structures.

√ To help group members open up and share personal temptation areas for the sake of sharing the load of the temptation.

GETTING ACQUAINTED   20–30 minutes

Have a group member read aloud **The Dragon of Temptation.** Then choose one of the following activities to help create a more comfortable, nonthreatening atmosphere.

Excuses, Excuses, Excuses

In this section we will discuss the temptations that are faced by group members in certain roles. The point of these questions is to get a look at how we all face very real temptations in our lives. We want to encourage people to see the pitfalls of their roles or occupations.

Pocket Principle

1 The Freedom to Pass Rule—Every group member deserves the freedom to pass on a question if he or she does not want to answer it. Never question the motives of the one passing.

GAINING INSIGHT   30–35 minutes

Recognizing Temptation
Have a group member read Galatians 5:19-21 and Ephesians 5:5. Then discuss the following questions.

☐ **How would you classify the areas of sin in the Galatians passage? See if you can classify them into four categories.** (The four broad categories of sin are sexual—sexual immorality, impurity, debauchery; religious—idolatry and witchcraft; relational—hatred, discord, jealousy, fits of rage, selfish ambition, dissensions, factions and envy; indulgence—drunkenness and orgies.)

☐ **What other category might you add from Ephesians 5:5?** (We can also add the category of greed from Ephesians 5:5. These five areas pretty well characterize the human experience of sin.)

☐ **Is there a particular item in these passages that is unknown to you or not defined well in your mind? If so, write it down and look it up in a dictionary.** (Perhaps the only sin that needs to be further defined is *debauchery*, which is an "extreme indulgence in sensuality" according to *Webster's New Collegiate Dictionary*.)

☐ **In what way is each of these sins a perversion of something that is good?** (The sexual category—God intended human beings to be sexual, and He provided marriage as the appropriate avenue for expressing sexual desires. The religious category—As spiritual beings, God intended us to enjoy the created order, but people deify what is earthly. The relational category—Anger carried to an unhealthy extreme becomes retribution, bitterness, and hatred; discord becomes bitter disputes; disagreements become personal and evolve into dissensions and factions. The indulgence category—Desire for pleasure goes to the extreme of drunkenness and orgies.)

Read Matthew 4:1-11 and discuss the following questions.

☐ **What is the setting for this temptation?** (desert)

106

❑ **In what way is the setting here in contrast with the setting of Adam and Eve?** (Adam and Eve had the best possible setting to not sin. Yet even in the surroundings of paradise they sinned. Jesus' situation in the desert was far worse, but He remained true to God's plan.)

❑ **What motivated Jesus to be in the wilderness at this point in His life?** (Notice how Jesus was led into the temptations by the Holy Spirit.)

❑ **In the first temptation Satan urged Jesus to change the stones to be bread. Why would this be a temptation for Jesus at this time?** (He was hungry, so the temptation to turn stones to bread was real.)

❑ **What does Jesus' response tell you about the way Jesus used His power for His own needs?** (Jesus did not take matters into His own hands but relied upon His Father for provision.)

❑ **In the second temptation, the devil challenged Jesus to use His power to draw a large following. How did Jesus respond to this temptation?** (He did not need to test God's Word in order for it to be effective and true.)

❑ **In what way did Jesus show that He will trust in God's plan and that He doesn't need to test God's word?** (Jesus showed that He trusted God's plan by steadfastly going to the cross. In Gethsemane, He prayed that His suffering would pass from Him, but His ultimate commitment was to do the Father's will.)

❑ **In the third temptation, Jesus was urged to gain access to ruling the kingdom by worshiping Satan. How did Jesus respond to this aspect of temptation, and what was the root of the issue?** (Jesus was tempted to gain the kingdom through improper means — by worshiping Satan as opposed to going through with death on the cross. Nevertheless, Jesus responded by declaring His allegiance to the Father and to Him only.)

Point out that Jesus drew upon the Scriptures from Deuteronomy as a weapon against the assaults of Satan. The Scriptures declare what is true and right, and they are the only measure of what is morally permissible.

Have two group members read 1 Corinthians 10:13 and Colossians 3:5. Explain that in 1 Corinthians, Paul states that we have some recourse in our dealing with temptation. First of all, God will not allow us to be tempted beyond what we are able and, secondly, He will provide a way of escape for those times when the temptation seems too great. We do have a choice in the midst of temptation.

Colossians 3:5 suggests that we are to "put to death" those things which are sinful. Paul urged the Colossians to realize that they no longer had to succumb to temptation as if there were no choice. The believer has died with Jesus so that the law of sin will no longer hold sway over the believer.

The overwhelming power of sin is gone. It can still tempt, but through Christ's work on the cross, we can overcome it.

GROWING BY DOING   15–20 minutes

Attacking The Dragon
We can help each other in attacking this dragon by talking about areas of sin and how to handle them. Use the following questions to facilitate sharing.

- ❏ **How does God provide the strength necessary to be under specific areas of temptation?**
- ❏ **How can God provide specific means of escape?**
- ❏ **How does a decision to deny sin's hold on us help in particular areas of sin?**
- ❏ **Does idleness have a role as well?**

Sometimes simply asking someone else to help hold us accountable is the most appropriate way of handling temptation. It could be a very helpful exercise to ask the group to offer such suggestions on a theoretical basis. We are not asking that people share their deepest sins, but we can ask them what such temptations to sin would be in their own environments.

GOING THE SECOND MILE   5–10 minutes

Challenge group members to complete this section on their own. Trying to decide whether you should play a part in holding someone accountable is tricky business. It is not enough to simply assume that we have such a role. More helpful is the situation where we have been asked to play such a role in someone's life. If such a situation exists, then we can exercise this aspect of accountability.

GROWING AS A LEADER

Perhaps there is no greater role that a leader plays than that of model. Modeling correct behavior and attitudes speaks louder than any words shared in the context of a meeting. Were you able to model your own need for accountability and your desire to be released from a sinful tendency? Determine to be a model of openness to God as you continue through these sessions.

FOUR

Defeating Discouragement

When most of us get into situations that we find terribly discouraging, we often have a hard time seeing our way through those situations. In this session, we will examine the life of the Prophet Elijah to see how we might take steps to deal with discouragement in our own lives.

Elijah did some great things for God. He was perhaps the greatest of all the prophets. When Jesus' glory was revealed on the Mount of Transfiguration, Moses and Elijah were present with Him. Symbolically, Moses represented the Law and Elijah represented the prophets. So we might be tempted to think that such a great man would never experience discouragement.

However, the confidence Elijah gained on Mount Carmel quickly dissolved to fear and discouragement as he fled from Queen Jezebel's death squads. In 1 Kings, we discover him in the pits, trying to deal with his fears and discouragement.

As **Group Leader** of this small group experience, *you* have a choice as to which elements will best fit your group, your style of leadership, and your purposes. After you examine the **Session Objectives**, select the activities under each heading with which to begin your community building. You have many choices.

SESSION OBJECTIVES

✓ To get acquainted by talking about what gives us times of discouragement.

✓ To listen as others open up their lives to the group.

✓ To learn how God reached out to Elijah in his time of need.

✓ To realize how we are vulnerable for an attack of discouragement.

✓ To decide how to defend ourselves against the tendency to become discouraged.

✓ To encourage one another with the tools God gives to fight discouragement.

GETTING ACQUAINTED   20–30 minutes

Have a group member read aloud **The Dragon of Discouragement.** Then choose one of the following activities to help create a more comfortable, nonthreatening atmosphere.

Defining Discouragement

Give group members the opportunity to define *discouragement* for themselves. Some of their definitions may be humorous while others may share deeper thoughts of depression.

Pocket Principle

1 In some instances you may come across a person who has deep, personal problems which require professional help. Do not be afraid to ask a group member who presents a very difficult problem during the session to wait until after the study to discuss his or her problem. Then you may be able to direct the person to a pastor or counselor for more specific help. You may want to offer prayer immediately, but specific counseling help should be given by a qualified counselor.

GAINING INSIGHT   30–35 minutes

Scripture Study

You may decide to have group members skim the story of Elijah and the prophets of Baal in 1 Kings 18. Or you may want to summarize the story to set the scene for Elijah's discouragement. Be sure to point out that Elijah ran ahead of Ahab all the way to Jezreel. Therefore, he was physically tired and more subject to discouragement (1 Kings 18:46).

Have the group review the following Scriptures and describe some of the things that caused Elijah to become discouraged:

❏ **1 Kings 19:1-2** (He was threatened by his enemies.)

❏ **1 Kings 19:3-5** (Under threat of death, he was lost in self-pity and longed to die.)

❏ **1 Kings 19:8-10** (He went to Mount Horeb [where God had appeared to Moses] in hopes of finding God. This was like hoping for the good old days even though God had already demonstrated His presence and power in Elijah's life.)

Now, have the group review the following Scriptures and determine what God did to help Elijah through this period of discouragement.

❏ **1 Kings 19:5-7** (God provided physical nourishment for Elijah.)

❏ **1 Kings 19:9-10** (God dealt gently by speaking to Elijah even though Elijah complained about God's treatment of him.)

❏ **1 Kings 19:11-13** (God reminded Elijah of His power and presence.)

❏ **1 Kings 19:14-18** (God showed Elijah that his self-pity was not warranted. There were many Israelites who remained faithful to the living God. God gave Elijah a practical plan of action to get him out of discouragement.)

112

❑ **1 Kings 19:19-21** (God gave Elijah a partner, someone to share the burden.)

GROWING BY DOING   15–20 minutes

Attacking The Dragon
In this section, group members will identify patterns of their own discouragement. In this way, they will be able to draw upon God's power and the encouragement of others. Urge group members to think about what will help them most in the midst of discouragement.

GOING THE SECOND MILE   5–10 minutes

Challenge group members to complete this section on their own. This is a time for action to help the discouraged. Encourage group members to establish a course of action to actively encourage others and to take the appropriate steps to draw upon God's help for themselves.

GROWING AS A LEADER

Did you ever notice feeling either encouraged or discouraged after a small group meeting? It's easy to personalize this evaluation and decide that we are responsible for the session going well or failing. Sometimes we are too close to the situation for an objective evaluation. In this session, we studied how God gave Elijah a partner at a time of discouragement. Is it possible to enlist a group member to help you with each session? Is there a time when you can get together with that person to evaluate the group meetings?

FIVE

Lifted Up From Hopelessness

Paul characterized our lives as having a treasure in jars of clay. Clay pots are not usually very attractive. They break. They have flaws. Pots of clay do not call attention to themselves, but strictly serve as vessels. And such is life. Though we encounter difficulties and feel our "earthenness," we are to perform the tasks that God asks of us.

In the midst of such circumstances, God is able to show His power and glory through our weaknesses. In fact, one might argue that it is through our weaknesses that God is seen the most. Paul said, "When I am weak, then I am strong" (2 Corinthians 12:10).

Yet we strive to feel strong at every point. We want to be perceived as self-sufficient. We want others to look and be convinced that we are capable and competent in what we do. We want to be valued by society, our churches, and our families.

So many times, however, we are disappointed in our performances, and our disappointment leads to a sense of hopelessness. Inside, we know we can't do things on our own, so we are confirmed in that hopelessness rather than challenged to rid ourselves of despair.

114

In 2 Corinthians 4:7-18, Paul showed us how to defeat the dragon of hopelessness. By looking beyond ourselves, we can know the richness of a life that is focused on the eternal, rather than on the temporal.

As **Group Leader** of this small group experience, *you* have a choice as to which elements will best fit your group, your style of leadership, and your purposes. After you examine the **Session Objectives**, select the activities under each heading with which to begin your community building.

SESSION OBJECTIVES

- √ To get acquainted by sharing some of the hopes and dreams of those in the group.
- √ To listen as others open up their lives to the group.
- √ To discern what Paul experienced that gave him hope and purpose.
- √ To help group members gain Paul's perspective on hardships.
- √ To encourage others to identify areas of hardship and concern and point them to God as our hope.
- √ To enable group members to recall verses from Scripture or songs that help us to remember our Christian hope.

GETTING ACQUAINTED   15–20 minutes

Have a group member read aloud **The Dragon of Hopelessness**. Then choose one of the following activities to help create a more comfortable, nonthreatening atmosphere.

I Wish . . .
This section will allow group members to get a glimpse of the special desires they have for the future. Some of these wishes will be pipe dreams with little hope of becoming realities. But it is fun to hear what group members would do if given the opportunity. Encourage the group to listen and get a picture of some of the inner desires of others.

115

GAINING INSIGHT   35–40 minutes

Scripture Study

Life is not always simple or enjoyable. We are confronted with those things which remind us of the pervading sinfulness of sin or the decay of life. As such, we need a glimpse beyond ourselves. We need the sure hope which Paul recognized and communicated in 2 Corinthians 4:7-18. After reading 2 Corinthians 4:17-18, discuss the following questions.

❑ **How could having meaning and purpose in life combat hopelessness?** (Many times people who are discouraged say that they have nothing to live for. A purpose in life urges us to go on and fulfill that purpose, to accomplish that goal. If we are convinced of the worth of a goal, we can commit ourselves to achieving it because the goal is more important than our own selfish desires.)

❑ **How do you know that Paul knew what it was like to encounter great difficulties as he worked and ministered to other people?** (Paul's role was one of messenger. He brought a message of hope and reconciliation to the world. Yet he was not often appreciated. In fact, many times he endured harsh treatment such as imprisonment, arrests, beatings, pursuit by his enemies, etc.)

❑ **How did Paul qualify his list of experiences in verses 8-9 to indicate what had not happened as a result of encountering difficulties?** (Paul explained that he struggled with his difficulties, but he did not buckle under the hardships and lose heart.)

❑ **Rephrase the principle found in verses 10-11 that describes how we might be able to see limitations or difficulties as positive times in our lives.** (The principle mentioned in verses 10-11 is that weakness is OK because it shows the greatness of Jesus. Paul's relationship with Jesus was intensified by his weakness. Paul understood that it is in difficult times that many can see Jesus working within us.)

❑ **What specifically was Paul's hope as mentioned in verses 13-14?** (Paul's hope was one of resurrection. To

116

be present with Jesus in eternal glory was far greater than the suffering Paul faced on earth.)

❑ **According to verse 16, this hope should lead us to what experience or attitude? In what way do our present circumstances make this a difficult attitude to have?** (The hope that we are given should lead us to an experience of daily renewal in the midst of decay. God can renew us spiritually when we are in the midst of difficulty.)

❑ **According to verse 18, how can we make this attitude a definite part of our lives?** (We can fix our eyes on this unseen reality to gain hope and encouragement for the days ahead.)

GROWING BY DOING   15–20 minutes

Attacking The Dragon
During this time ask group members to talk about how they can identify with Paul's statements about being persecuted, perplexed, etc.

Close with sentence prayers. Prayer helps us look beyond ourselves to the hope and help Jesus gives. Encourage group members to share their concerns in a few sentences in order to alleviate one or two people from dominating this prayer time.

GOING THE SECOND MILE   5–10 minutes

Challenge group members to complete this section on their own. One option for your group during this section is to ask group members to read verses which recall the certain hope the believer has. These can be read aloud as a challenge to see beyond this life to the unseen reality Paul spoke about.

GROWING AS A LEADER

One thing that a leader finds out quickly is that personal involvement in others' lives is just as important as the knowl-

117

edge that the leader may have. During this session on lifting people up from despair and leading them to hope, examine your own hopes for the people in your group. Are you committed to helping them have the hope that they will grow in their commitment to each other and to the Lord? Are you in leadership for the right reason—to serve them? Can you demonstrate your commitment to them by consistently praying for them?

SIX

From Doubt to Conviction

Paul said that he endured dangers almost every hour for the sake of Christ. "I die every day—I mean that, brothers—just as surely as I glory over you in Christ Jesus our Lord. If I fought wild beasts in Ephesus for merely human reasons, what have I gained? If the dead are not raised, 'Let us eat and drink, for tomorrow we die'" (1 Corinthians 15:31-34).

Paul's absolute conviction regarding Christ's resurrection enabled him to go into situations which might be terrifying. He was able to face his enemies and those who challenged him because he knew the resurrected Christ.

There is no question that our world presents to us fearful possibilities. As we approach other people with the message of the Gospel, we often fear rejection and ridicule. We can be sure that Paul faced similar situations, but he did it with such conviction that rejection and ridicule meant little to him.

In this session, we hope to capture Paul's level of conviction in order to dispel our doubts. If we are filled with doubt, our lives are powerless and pathetic. But when we are filled with conviction about who Christ is, what He has done, and what He promises, our lives will be dynamic and powerful.

As **Group Leader** of this small group experience, *you* have a choice as to which elements will best fit your group, your style of leadership, and your purposes. After you examine the **Session Objectives**, select activities under each heading.

SESSION OBJECTIVES

√ To get acquainted by discussing what we think will happen in our lives in the future.

√ To listen as others open up their lives to the group.

√ To examine the difference between living lives based on doubt or based on conviction.

√ To learn how to live with conviction based on the disciples' experiences with Jesus.

√ To decide how to attack the lingering doubts in our lives.

√ To remind others of the truth of the Gospel and the benefits of living in the light of that truth.

GETTING ACQUAINTED   20–30 minutes

Have a group member read aloud **The Dragon of Doubt**. Then choose one of the following activities to help create a more comfortable, nonthreatening atmosphere.

Shadows of Doubts
In this section, we will look into what group members are planning to have happen in the next day or week. This activity will expand our view of the lives of other group members. Encourage everyone to really give us a glimpse of their expectations. We also introduce the concept of doubt versus conviction.

GAINING INSIGHT   30–35 minutes

Scripture Study
In this section, we will give group members the same assurances that the disciples had to live a life full of conviction and not of doubt.

120

After reading the two passages, discuss the following questions.

❑ **Based on Luke 24:37-42, what evidence did Jesus give of His resurrection?** (He stood among them and spoke, v. 36. He dispelled the idea that He was a ghost or vision by showing the disciples His feet and hands to confirm the physical nature of His Resurrection, vv. 38-39. He ate to further demonstrate He was risen, v. 42.)

❑ **In Luke 24:36, Jesus said, "Peace be with you." How does certainty of Christ's resurrection lead us to peace?** (Knowing that Christ's Resurrection is real helps us have hope of God's care both now and in the life to come. The life of the Christian is the only way to have true wholeness.)

❑ **What are things that we face in the future that require a life full of conviction rather than doubt?** (We face opposition from unbelievers regarding our faith. We confront times when circumstances are not pleasant, and we are faced with the death of loved ones as well as our own deaths.)

❑ **How do these facts concerning Christ's resurrection help us when we are given the command to be Christ's witnesses?** (The knowledge of what Christ has done in conquering death should lead us to new boldness in sharing the Scriptures. We have the assurance of an actual, not imagined, resurrection of Christ.)

❑ **Jesus promised that we might receive power through the Holy Spirit. How does this help in our proclamation of the Gospel to other people?** (In our own selves we are not able to bring about true change in another's religious beliefs. But God can bring about change, giving power and opportunity through the Holy Spirit.)

❑ **What do you know about the Book of Acts that would indicate that the disciples changed from doubt to conviction regarding their understanding of Jesus after His death?** (Peter and Paul, in particular, were transformed when they fully recognized the validity of the

Resurrection. Peter went from denial of knowing Christ to preaching to thousands. Paul went from persecutor to proclaimer after Jesus' appearance to him.)

❑ **In John 20:19 how would you characterize the attitude and behavior of the disciples? What prompted this?** (They were huddled behind a locked door. They feared the authorities might search them out as followers of Jesus.)

❑ **Compare the disciples' response to Jesus' sudden appearance in John 20:19-20 with their response in Luke 24:37, 41.** (In Luke 24, the disciples were fearful and startled. In John 20, they were overjoyed with the Lord's presence.)

❑ **We often think that Thomas (often called "doubting Thomas") had a tremendous lack of faith. But would we be any different? How did Jesus answer Thomas' doubt in John 20:26-27?** (The disciple's experience is like our own. We probably would have questioned the possibility of resurrection prior to Christ's appearances after His death. Note how Jesus provided Thomas with actual physical evidence of His resurrection.)

❑ **What was Thomas' response to Jesus' actions?** (He responded by recognizing Jesus as his Lord and his God.)

❑ **Jesus apparently had us in mind when He said, "Blessed are those who have not seen and yet have believed" (John 20:29). How does Jesus' response to Thomas help us live lives of conviction?** (Jesus dealt gently with Thomas, recognizing the difficulty that Thomas may have had with the idea of resurreciton. We can take comfort and confidence in Christ's Resurrection because He was able to convince a skeptic like Thomas.)

❑ **According to John 20:31, why did God give us these evidences of Christ's miraculous power and His resurrection?** (That we might have life in the Son of God.)

GROWING BY DOING 15–20 minutes

Attacking The Dragon
Some people do not believe the Resurrection or the claims of Jesus. But such objections are easily answered. If someone complains that resurrections don't happen, we can counter with the statement that the Gospels are historical evidence that the Resurrection indeed did happen. For those who think that Jesus never died, we can show that this is ludicrous in light of the fact that the Romans were experts in putting people to death. The Gospels provide ample evidence to confront others with this life-giving message.

GOING THE SECOND MILE 5–10 minutes

Challenge group members to complete this section on their own. Encourage group members to look seriously at how they can translate their conviction into action. It may be an action to stand up against immoral actions at work or to witness in a bold way to someone.

GROWING AS A LEADER

Examine the structure of the group meeting time. Ask the following questions:

- ❏ Did I start on time?
- ❏ Did I allow sufficient time for **Getting Acquainted**?
- ❏ Have I been sensitive to needs/concerns of group members?
- ❏ Have I moved people along even if we didn't get finished with every question?
- ❏ Did I make sure we addressed the application section, **Growing By Doing**?
- ❏ Did I break up the group to facilitate sharing?
- ❏ Did I end on time?

These questions will lead you to be aware of the importance of structuring the meeting to both facilitate sharing and to attend to important aspects of small group life.

123

SEVEN

Shedding Bitterness

We all have known times of disappointment, times when our dreams have been shattered, our relationships have been stretched, and our circumstances difficult. We also know people who can recall in great detail all of the difficulties that they have had in their lives, and they are able to relate the disappointments with venomous scorn and poison words. No one likes being around a bitter person. Perhaps we live with such a person, or are closely associated with that kind of a man or woman, or perhaps we realize all too well that our circumstances have led us to become bitter.

"Hope deferred makes the heart sick, but a longing fulfilled is a tree of life," says the writer of Proverbs 13:12. There are so many people whose hearts are sick and find themselves in a disappointing season of their lives. But we can help them and us move beyond revenge and poisonous talk to the place of fulfillment and with the confidence that we can trust God with our every circumstance.

As **Group Leader** of this small group experience, *you* have a choice as to which elements will best fit your group, your style of leadership, and your purposes. After you examine the **Session Objectives**, select the activities under each heading with which to begin your community building.

SESSION OBJECTIVES

√ To get acquainted by discussing the meaningful relationships group members have had.

√ To listen as others open up their lives to the group.

√ To gain insight from the example of Joseph so that we might live lives free from the bitterness that is so prevalent in relationships today.

√ To help group members identify a disappointing relationship and plan how to relieve the bitterness that may characterize that relationship.

√ To lead group members to pray for one another for these relationships.

√ To encourage group members to admonish one another to make appropriate steps in reconciling relationships.

GETTING ACQUAINTED   25–30 minutes

Have a group member read aloud **The Dragon of Bitterness.** Then choose one of the following activities to help create a more comfortable, nonthreatening atmosphere.

Significant Relationships

This section should be very easy. We can simply open up a group discussion about a key relationship we have had and why it was successful. This should be very encouraging to the group as they stress the positive aspects of personal relationships.

GAINING INSIGHT   30–35 minutes

Scripture Study

After reading Genesis 37:3-4, 19-24, discuss the following questions.

❑ **Why do you think Joseph's brothers were moved to take such drastic action against him?** (Joseph may not have been the most tactful person in dealing with his brothers. He had a tendency to brag even though he was one of the youngest.)

❑ **What do you think marked their relationship with Joseph?** (They were envious of Joseph and didn't appreciate the way their father favored him.)

❑ **How did they handle their own disappointments and jealousies?** (They probably had some right to be angry, but they channeled their anger into bitterness and not into constructive relationship building.)

❑ **What steps do you think were taken that allowed bitterness to take such deep root in Joseph's brothers?** (Step 1—Favoritism on the part of Joseph's father, vv. 3-4. Step 2—Lavish gifts given to Joseph but not to the other sons, v. 3. Step 3—Joseph's dreams of superiority over his brothers, v. 19.)

Read Genesis 39:1-6 and discuss how Joseph handled this very disappointing situation. Point out that Joseph's life was far from easy once he was sold into slavery. Circumstances certainly did not go his way.

Next read Genesis 39:19-23 and talk about how you think Joseph reacted to this new situation in prison. Then read Genesis 41:15-24, 39-43 and 45:3-8. Discuss the following questions.

❑ **After all his bad experiences, how do you think Joseph felt about Pharaoh's decision to put him in charge of Egypt?** (Joseph must have been gratified to finally have his efforts and responsibility recognized. As a follower of God, he undoubtedly felt the hand of God guiding his life.)

❑ **What do you think made the difference between the way Joseph responded to the difficult circumstances that resulted from his broken relationship with his brothers and the way the brothers responded to Joseph?** (Joseph had an abiding confidence that he could be faithful to his calling no matter where God had placed him. He seemed to know the principle that God works through all situations for our good [Romans 8:28].)

❑ **How would you summarize Joseph's strategy for handling bitterness?** (He responded to unfortunate circumstances by serving God wherever he found himself.

126

He didn't wallow in self-pity or thoughts of revenge. He saw God supervising even the distasteful times of his life, and he chose not to retaliate for harm.)

GROWING BY DOING   15–20 minutes

Attacking The Dragon
Major disappointments and difficult circumstances are probably present in the lives of many of your group members. It's good to talk about each of the disappointing relationships that group members may share. Then we may offer prayer for reconciliation and ideas for making reconciliation a reality.

GOING THE SECOND MILE   5–10 minutes

Challenge group members to complete this section on their own. Encourage them to evaluate where the group is at and how they can be more helpful to one another.

Ask group members to seriously evaluate how they can take personal steps for restoring relationships. Be aware that some may need counseling to do that.

GROWING AS A LEADER

Focus on the preparation that you are doing prior to each session. Have you been able to set aside sufficient time for study? Here are some steps for preparation:

❑ Read the Bible passage several times with several different translations.

❑ Examine the options for **Getting Acquainted** to see which activities best fit the needs of your group.

❑ Answer the questions in **Gaining Insights** without referring to the Leader's Guide. Then compare your answers with those in the Guide.

❏ Highlight those questions which struck you as important for your group if time should run short.
❏ Apply the study to your own life before the session.

EIGHT

Handling Failure

Failure can be devastating. To not gain the success one expects in a profession or sport hurts our self-esteem. We want to be seen as self-sufficient, in control of our own destinies, without limitations. But most of us know better. We know we will have times of failure and disappointment. We know we will have to face up to the fact that we have not measured up.

John Wesley made a trip to Georgia to try to have an impact on the people in the New World, but he returned to Britain sensing failure. Yet God was not finished with him. Wesley formed a movement that impacted the world. He did not allow failure to shackle him. He pressed on to find God's purpose in his life and pursued that purpose relentlessly.

Failure and disappointment can be debilitating. How many of us know people who have allowed past failures to hinder future accomplishments. People look at past failures in relationships and sometimes avoid future involvement in others' lives. Some people allow past failures in business to cripple future endeavors. But God intends for us to move beyond failure to depend on His grace and goodness to achieve His will for our lives. In this session, we will look at the dragon of failure.

As **Group Leader** of this small group experience, *you* have a choice as to which elements will best fit your group, your

129

style of leadership, and your purposes. After you examine the **Session Objectives**, select the activities under each heading with which to begin your community building.

SESSION OBJECTIVES

√ To get acquainted by helping group members share things they really do well and not so well.

√ To listen as others open up their lives to the group.

√ To learn how Jesus dealt so compassionately with Peter after his dreadful failure.

√ To help group members face failure in a way that leads them on to success and not to despair or discouragement.

√ To lead group members to ask for and gain forgiveness from God and others.

√ To encourage group members to examine ways of affirming each other in the successes we have had and not dwell on the failures.

GETTING ACQUAINTED   25–30 minutes

Have a group member read aloud **The Dragon of Failure.** Then choose one of the following activities to help create a more comfortable, nonthreatening atmosphere.

What I Do Best

This is a chance for group members to share the things that they really do well with the rest of the group. We gain insight through this exercise into what group members like to do. We will also find that we may be able to draw upon the strengths of various members of the group at different times in the life of the group.

We'll also spend some time talking about things we do poorly. This is not intended to parade group members' weaknesses before others. Rather, it is to introduce the idea that we all fail and respond differently to failure.

GAINING INSIGHT   30–35 minutes

Scripture Study

Two sections of Scripture are included here. Luke 22:54-62 provides us with background and the episode of Peter's failure. John 21:15-22 shows us how Jesus restored Peter's status and position. After a group member reads these two passages aloud, discuss the following questions.

❑ **Describe the pressures that Peter might have felt when he was questioned about Jesus in Luke 22:54-62. What was the tone of Peter's responses?** (Certainly there are many reasons that Peter felt compelled to lie. He was scared, intimidated, and curious.)

❑ **How did Peter respond when he rejected Jesus for the third time and heard the rooster crow?** (When Peter couldn't come to the point of clearly acknowledging Jesus, he wept bitterly.)

❑ **In John 21:15-23 we find that Jesus graciously reached out to Peter in a way that restored Peter's position and assured him of Jesus' love. Why do you think that Jesus questioned Peter's love at this point?** (In asking Peter to feed the flock of God, Jesus showed His confidence in Peter's ability for the future regardless of his past performance.)

❑ **How do you think Peter felt about Jesus' questions?** (He probably felt very frustrated that Jesus would ask him the same question over and over.)

❑ **What is significant about the number of times that Jesus questioned Peter's love?** (Jesus reached out to Peter by asking him to state his love three times. Jesus was obviously giving Peter the chance to undo what he had done earlier.)

❑ **Why did Peter question Jesus about John? What was Jesus' response?** (Peter had enough to be concerned about in himself.)

❑ **What does this say about comparing both the performance and position of children of God?** (Jesus' admonition to Peter is for us as well. We have enough to take care of in ourselves to not worry about how God is treating others or how others are responding to Him.)

GROWING BY DOING   15–20 minutes

Attacking The Dragon
Talking about our own failures can be disconcerting. However, we can encourage others to talk about how to get beyond failures to carry on with life. In the case of failures toward people, we can go to them with repentance asking for reconciliation. The promise God gives us in 1 John 1:9 assures us of the restoration of our relationship with God.

GOING THE SECOND MILE   5–10 minutes

Challenge group members to complete this section on their own. It would be great at this point in the life of the group to take time to affirm the talents and abilities of the group members. You may want to ask group members to break down into groups of three to affirm each other.

GROWING AS A LEADER

This is an appropriate time to evaluate what God has done through you as a leader. You know of areas where you have failed and succeeded. Evaluate yourself in the following ways:

❏ Am I able to discern when to move the group along in discussion?
❏ Am I sensitive to particular needs in the group?
❏ Am I able to follow the session plan and be flexible in my time constraints?
❏ Am I being challenged in my own life?
❏ Am I growing in love and commitment to the other group members?
❏ Do I enjoy leading this group?
❏ Do others comment on my abilities and involvement?
❏ Do I sense the group being knit together in commitment?
❏ Is there a desire to continue meeting?
❏ Do I want to do more leading of this group?